FLYING AN UNARMED AUSTER FOR THE ROYAL ARTILLERY IN THE KOREAN WAR

Recollections of learning to fly as a Gunner Officer and flying in Hong Kong and Korea as an Air Observation Post Pilot

Lt Col Derek Jarvis (retd), RA, DFC, US Air Medal

Military History Publishing, an imprint of Books Express Publishing

© Derek Jarvis 2017

All rights reserved. No part of this publication may be reproduced, stored in a retrieval system, or transmitted in any form or by any means, electronic, mechanical, photocopying, recording or otherwise, without the prior written permission of the author.

Dedication

I am deeply indebted to my wife Anne and my son Simon, without whose help and encouragement this book would not have been written.

Derek Jarvis

Calne, Wiltshire

2015

Table of contents

List of illustrations   6

Foreword: Chris Hobson   11

Preface   13

Chapter 1   Introduction   15

Chapter 2   Learning to fly   21

Chapter 3   Flying in Hong Kong and on to Korea   27

Chapter 4   Joining the First Commonwealth Division   35

Chapter 5   Into action and continuing operations up to December 1951   43

Chapter 6   Continuing operations: from December 1951   51

Chapter 7   Counter-bombardment   57

Chapter 8   Operations to the end of 1952   65

Chapter 9   Three months as an Observation Post officer on the ground   79

Conclusion   90

Annex I: Extract from a report by the Divisional Counter-Bombardment Officer, Major Thomas RA   92

Annex II: Second report from the Divisional Counter-Bombardment Officer, Major Thomas RA   95

Annex III: Additional photographs   98

Glossary   113

List of illustrations

Chapter 2

Page 21: The de Havilland Tiger Moth

Page 23: The Link Trainer in the hangar at Booker

Page 24: The Auster Mark VI

Page 26: Nearly the end of my flying career

Chapter 3

Page 27: Hong Kong in 1950: Cricket Club to right of Hong Kong and Shanghai Bank

Page 30: Hiroshima; Iwakuni airfield

Page 31: The Dome: Ground Zero of the Atomic Bomb on Hiroshima

Page 32: Route from Iwakuni via Ashyia and Pusan to the 38th parallel

Page 33: Flying from Pusan to Seoul

Page 34: Tokchong strip: the aircraft can be seen between the huts and the camouflage nets

Additional photographs

Page 98: Mia Jima; Self at Iwakuni; Mia Jima, sacred island in the Inland Sea

Page 99: Tokchong strip

Page 100: Number 4 Section and supporting cast; Pilot briefing: self on left, Major Ronnie Gower and Captain John Crawshaw; Waiting for the Boss to do a bad landing: Captains Dick Corfield and Leslie Addington and self on right

Chapter 4

Page 35: A US Harvard T6 Mosquito on Fort George strip

Page 36: Daily maintenance

Page 37: 1903 AOP Flight September 1951: pilots in front row from left, Derek Jarvis, Terry Fitzgibbon, Dick Corfield, Ronnie Gower, Leslie Addington, Arthur Stewart-Cox

Page 38: A typical Korean village

Page 39: Operation Commando

List of illustrations   7

Page 40: Major Ronnie Gower receiving a "Mention In Dispatches" after Operation Commando

Page 41: Korea "The Land of the morning calm" … before the North Koreans and the Chinese destroyed it

Chapter 5

Page 42: Approximate front line from November to July 1953

Page 45: US Air OPs arrive on Fort George strip in L19s

Page 46: Pontoon bridge at Pintail; Bofors LAA guns of 11 Sphinx Battery RA guarding Pintail Bridge. Six months earlier, this battery had engaged Chinese infantry over open sights during the Gloucester's Imjin battle about four miles to the west. Soon after this picture was taken they converted to become a 4.2 inch Mortar Battery

Page 47: US Army Beaver and US Marine Corps Corsair. Corporal Parr RAF telling the Americans how to repair it

Page 48: Pilots' mess; Cookhouse area

Additional photographs

Page 101: General Ridgeway, General Van Fleet, Lieutenant General O'Daniel arriving at Fort George strip; Major-General Cassels briefing his masters on Operation Commando, 17 July 1951; Major-General Cassels and Lieutenant General O'Daniel; Corsair finally ready for take-off

Page 102: US Grumman Avenger landing and taking off from Fort George strip; Major-General Cassel's private aeroplane with RAF roundels and chauffeur, Captain Tony Wilson; Seoul city gateway; Korean woman making flour

Page 103: Joe Luscombe and I seem to have been invited in to the men's mess for a drink; LAC Howe and Gunner Price

Chapter 6

Page 55: Danny Kaye with Brigadier Pike, the Deputy Divisional Commander

Page 56: Concert party

Additional photograph

Page 103: An American entertainer, Brigadier Pike and Danny Kaye

Chapter 7

Page 57: Joe Luscombe in the crew room waiting for a sortie

8   List of illustrations

Page 59: This photo, taken from 6,000 feet, shows a single field gun in the centre of the photo and two medium four-gun positions in the top left-hand corner, and it shows how difficult they were to spot

Page 60: There are two gun positions in this photo

Page 61: There is one gun position in the centre of the photo

Page 62: Two photos of Chinese positions on point 169 in January 1952

Page 63: This photo shows the same position about two and a half months later. This third photo, from 2,000 feet, clearly shows the extensive trenches of an enemy platoon and company position on point 169 on the centre of the front. These hills were originally wooded, but were now completely bare, due to the constant bombardment of our shells and mortars

Chapter 8

Page 65: Bob Warner with me in the back seat visiting the US Air OPs on Projectile strip

Page 66: Farewell drinks party for Major-General Cassels, at Divisional Headquarters

Page 67: 1903 Flight early 1952: pilots from left, Bob Warner, Arthur Stewart-Cox, Ronnie Gower, Derek Jarvis, and John Crawshaw. Joe Luscombe had just been killed

Page 68: "Whirly Bird" Bell helicopter

Page 69: SAC Smith, engine mechanic. He kept my aircraft airworthy for over a year; Pilots' crew room

Pages 70–71: These oblique photos, which I took from 2,000 feet, show the Chinese forward positions in the centre of the divisional front. The Chinese anti-tank ditches can be seen at the bottom left of the pictures and the Chinese trenches are on top of all the bare hills. We supplied the divisional intelligence staff with photos such as these of the whole divisional front on a weekly basis

Page 72: Kiwi gunners getting into action in winter 1951; 2nd Royal Canadian Horse Artillery Regiment in action

Page 73: Iwo Jima airstrip; The RAAF Dakota and a Japanese 75-mm gun

Page 74: The airstrip on Momote near Manus in the Admiralty Group; bottom: loading before taking off for Townsville

Page 76: Point 227, Mathew, Luke and John; not a vestige of vegetation left

List of illustrations 9

Chapter 9

Page 79: Original 75 Observation Post; The new Observation Post

Pages 80–81: Aerial views of the enemy positions in front of me

Pages 82–83: Panoramic view from 75 Observation Post

Page 85: Major-General Jim Cassels presenting me with the DFC ribbon on Fort George airstrip

Page 86: A Centurion tank of the 8th Queen's Royal Irish Hussars, dug in near a company reserve position; Fox Troop, numbers two and four guns; the detachment operated in two halves, one commanded by the sergeant and the other by the bombardier, so that one half of the detachment was firing the gun whilst the other slept; their sleeping quarters can be seen in front of number two gun

Page 87: Number one gun of Fox Troop 13 Martinique Battery out of action for maintenance. The quads, or gun towing vehicles, and ammunition vehicles and drivers were back at B echelon and were only called up if the Battery had to move; the Troop command post was behind the guns and well dug into the side of a hill; orders were passed to the guns by a Tannoy system

Page 89: About to entrain at Tokchong: Aubrey Fielder, Gibbo, and Mike Hunter, the Medical Officer; On the train: Harry Pearson, Dougie Cook, Frank Ward, Peter Harrison

Additional photographs

Page 103: Derek Jarvis; Ronnie Gower

Page 104: Bob Warner; Arthur Stewart-Cox; Joe Luscombe and John Crawshaw; Gerry Joyce and Derek Jarvis; Brian Forward; Farewell drinks party for Major-General Cassels, at Divisional Headquarters

Page 105: New Commander in Chief General Mark Clark and guard of honour of the King's Shropshire Light Infantry; King's Shropshire Light Infantry; King's Own Scottish Borderers

Page 106: Divisional forward positions; battle maps

Page 107: Major-General Cassels briefing Selwyn Lloyd, General Van Fleet, Lord Alexander and General Clark; Selwyn Lloyd, Lord Alexander, Lieutenant-General O'Daniel; Guard of honour First Royal Canadian Regiment; War Office briefcases; Major-General Cassels and Lord Alexander outside 1903 Flight Headquarters

Page 108: Kawana, near Tokyo; Kawana Golf Club

10   List of illustrations

Pages 108–109: The sacred island of Mia Jima on the Inland Sea of Japan

Page 109: Touring Japan

Page 110: Right sector from the Observation Post; 1st King's front; 75 Observation Post at top right

Page 111: 11 and 12 Platoons of B Company 1st King's from 75 Observation Post; enemy positions on point 166 and point 75 in the background the other side of the Samichon valley; The reverse slope of the company position and Gunner Jones outside the Observation Post base; the OP party consisted of Gunners Jones, the signaller, McColl, the driver/batman, and Parfitt, the OP assistant

Page 112: Reverse slope of B Company position; 1st King's 3-inch mortars; Lieutenant-Colonel Jack Slade Powell; Captain John Painter E Troop, Major Tug Wilson Battery Commander, Captain Harry Pearson BK, and myself F Troop

Conclusion

Page 91: Miss Winifred Jarvis, my aunt, Captain Derek Jarvis, and Mr Michael Jarvis, my brother, at Buckingham Palace; the author receiving the US Air Medal at the United States Embassy in London

Foreword

To say that Derek Jarvis had an interesting and varied service career would be a gross understatement. There can't be many people who joined the Royal Air Force in 1943, transferred to the British Army in 1944 (due to the oversupply of aircrew), served with five different regiments within the space of five years and spent fourteen months flying over the front line during the Korean War.

After joining the Royal Artillery in 1948, Derek completed his training as an Air Observation Post Pilot in June 1950 and was posted to Malaya, flying the Auster light aircraft over the jungle in search of Communist insurgents during the Malayan Emergency. After gaining much valuable experience in Malaya and Hong Kong, Derek's unit, 1903 Flight, was loaded onto HMS Unicorn and sailed off to join the First Commonwealth Division, which was fighting alongside the United States and other Allied forces in Korea. 1903 Flight was an unusual organisation, being officially a Royal Air Force unit but manned by Army Gunner Pilots and maintained by a mixture of RAF and Army groundcrew.

Britain's air contribution to the Korean War was limited and fragmentary, consisting mainly of maritime patrols by Sunderland flying boats and Fleet Air Arm fighter-bomber squadrons flying from the Royal Navy's aircraft carriers. These were supplemented by exchange postings, whereby a small number of RAF pilots flew operationally with the US Air Force or the Royal Australian Air Force. Perhaps the least known of Britain's air operations in Korea was the sterling work performed by 1903 Flight, and so this book is a most valuable addition to the literature of the Korean War.

The work of this small Air Observation Post unit in Korea was in many respects similar to the battlefield reconnaissance performed by pilots and observers flying BE2s and RE8s over the Western Front during the First World War. Both involved flying flimsy, fairly basic aircraft; both were exposed to enemy ground fire for long periods; and both were living under quite primitive conditions. The work they performed in both wars may not have been seen as glamorous or high profile, but it was invaluable to the ground forces they supported, particularly to the artillery.

Derek's account of life and work in the Imjin River valley gives a unique insight into the difficulties faced by his unit when performing its vital task in the face of extreme weather, extreme terrain and an extremely determined enemy. The unit was based at an airstrip called Fort George, which sounds much grander than it was, but it also operated from other strips that were only just long enough to get an Auster in and out with a reasonable chance of success. A not-uncommon problem in wartime was the difficulty experienced in Korea in maintaining aircraft at forward bases, and the problems of obtaining spare parts, sometimes from as far away as Hong Kong or Singapore. Coupled with the problems of living in inadequate accommodation and surviving on fairly basic food, the hardships experienced by the aircrew and groundcrew of 1903 Flight can be well appreciated.

Derek Jarvis has given us a really valuable insight into events that happened half way across the world over sixty years ago. This book is not just a personal narrative but a detailed description and commentary on the tactics, organisation, equipment and day-to-day operations of an aspect of air warfare that has never received its fair share of attention. The fact that the book is written in a style which makes it a joy to read is an added bonus.

Chris Hobson

Chief Librarian, Joint Services Command and Staff College, Watchfield

Preface

In Korea, in the middle of January 1952, I found myself, as a 26-year-old Captain in the Royal Artillery, flying a small fabric covered unarmed Auster aircraft at about 6,000 feet and some 3 miles behind the Chinese lines at a numbing temperature of minus 46°. I was on a routine reconnaissance of the divisional front and was then hotly engaged by Chinese light anti-aircraft guns, which luckily did me no damage.

I then spotted a large number of Chinese soldiers out in the open, and, moving up to the front line, I engaged them with all seventy-two of the 25-pounder guns of the Commonwealth Divisional Artillery with air-burst shells, which certainly dispersed them, and probably caused considerable casualties.

So this book is a story of how I learnt to fly, and eventually ended up doing this in the Korean War as a Royal Artillery Air Observation Post Pilot.

Derek Jarvis

1
Introduction

I first acquired the ambition to fly when still at school in 1942. Specifically, I wished to become a Spitfire pilot. I volunteered for the Royal Air Force (RAF) and passed the necessary medical and flying aptitude tests and was attested as an aircraftman class II in October 1943, aged 17½. Unfortunately, the RAF had too many aircrew under training at this time, so I was put on deferred service for nine months, at which time I started to work on a farm near Plymouth. A decoy oil-fired town had been built on the farm near the River Yealm, about nine miles east of Plymouth, and on many nights the German Air Force mistakenly bombed these decoys. My first job in the morning was to take out a percheron draught horse with a large metal scoop with wooden handles, and I would spend the first hour of the morning filling in all the bomb craters. At this time I joined the Air Training Corps and became a flight sergeant, and at the same time I joined the Home Guard, so I had two uniforms. I suppose I was another Private Pike as in *Dad's Army*! The platoon had in fact two Private Pikes, and one night the two of us set up the Lewis gun on the platoon commander's lawn and managed to destroy a Junkers 88, which had already been damaged over Plymouth, and was caught in the searchlight cones. We managed to shoot it down into the sea in Mothecombe Bay, just east of Plymouth.

During this period I attended a fortnight's annual camp with the Air Training Corps at RAF Mountbatten in Plymouth. It was here that I got my first real flying experience. The Sunderland flying-boats were short of air gunners, so, at just eighteen, I manned the rear four-gun turret on a ten-hour anti-submarine patrol over the Atlantic. Luckily, my almost total lack of training as an air gunner was not put to the test.

In April 1944 I was fully enlisted into the RAF and did my initial training in London, living in hotels in Regent's Park and training at Lord's cricket ground, and then latterly at Torquay. Having completed this, I expected to start Elementary Flying Training School, but instead I was put on a six-month university course for an inter BSc degree at King's College, Aberdeen. Though undergraduates, we were put into uniform and had to march to and from the university every day.

Having finished at Aberdeen, I had expected to start flying training, but yet again it didn't happen, and I found myself along with the many thousands of fully trained aircrew and trainee aircrew at the Royal Air Force station at Sheerness on the Isle of Sheppey. The RAF, at the time of the D-day landings in June 1944, had nearly two crews for every aircraft they possessed, and nearly four crews under training, like myself. Luckily, the air casualties on the Continent were not as high as expected, so the RAF ended up with far more aircrew than they actually needed. We were then all put through a re-grading sausage machine. The country was extremely short of manpower at this time and so we were all sent off to other occupations. I was told that as my name began with J, I was to be a Bevin Boy, digging coal. I managed to get an interview with a squadron leader. He asked me why I wanted to see him, and I said that, though I did not wish to dig coal, I would do as I was told, but that I would much rather become a soldier. He asked me why, and I said that my father was then fighting his second World War as a soldier, and that I would rather follow in his footsteps. To my great surprise he agreed, and took me off one list and put me on another. A fortnight later, I was a rifleman in the King's Royal Rifle Corps doing nine months' basic training for one of the motor battalions which supported the armoured regiments. The Army could not cope with this sudden influx of unexpected manpower and ran out of uniforms, so during the day we were wearing brown denims and a brown hat with a rifle, and in the evening we were allowed out in York, still wearing our RAF blue uniforms. I was in a platoon of thirty men, two-thirds of whom I had been with in the RAF at the University of Aberdeen. This seemed to be the end of any hopes I ever had of flying, so I settled down to soldiering.

I completed the first nine months' intensive training and became a fully trained rifleman, and also a driver / vehicle mechanic on the Bedford 15-cwt truck. At this time I was posted to the Far East to fight the Japanese. However, I had also just passed the War Office Selection Board for a commission, and therefore did not go to the Far East, but instead was sent to an officer cadet training unit at Sandhurst, and in April 1946 I was commissioned into the Queen's Royal Regiment and posted to Pola in Yugoslavia. After the war, Tito and his partisans, our allies during the conflict, occupied Pola, which was then Italy's second-largest naval base, and proceeded to oppress the majority of its habitants. A British brigade was ordered to invade Yugoslavia from Trieste and to restore law and order. I joined the brigade in time to see the last of the three Queen's battalions disbanding, and overnight I found myself as a young officer in the Second Battalion of the Monmouthshire Regiment, guarding this enormous naval base, which had been utterly destroyed by the American Air Force at the end of the war.

Very soon the Monmouthshire Regiment was also disbanded in Italy, and I then joined the First Battalion of the Royal Northumberland Fusiliers in Trieste, and then in Tripoli in Cyrenaica, and subsequently the Second Battalion in Gibraltar. Whilst there, I was ordered to take my platoon to sea on a tank landing craft. My sealed orders from the Governor of Gibraltar were that I was to find a certain ship in the Atlantic approaches, arrest her on the high seas, and then bring her to Gibraltar. We found the ship, which was a small coaster from the United States with a 20° list as the coal ballast had shifted during a gale. Having successfully boarded her, I placed one armed guard on the anchor, another in the engine room and a third on the bridge and told the captain to sail the ship to Gibraltar. After a certain amount of persuasion he eventually did this. The ship was bound for southern France to collect Jewish refugees, and was then going to attempt to run the Royal Navy's blockade and finally beach in Palestine.

At this time I was granted a regular commission in the Royal Artillery and, after a six-month conversion course in Palestine, I joined 75 Battery of 48 Field Regiment Royal Artillery in Jerusalem. Here I did my very first shoot as a gun position officer with four 25-pounder guns firing live ammunition against some 500 Jews and 500 Arabs fighting each other on the Jerusalem/Latrun road. The shoot was conducted by a gunner air observation post (OP) pilot in an Auster light observation aircraft, which again rekindled my ideas about flying.

Early on the morning of 14 May 1948, 75 Battery left Jerusalem, followed by 2 Infantry Brigade. Interestingly, my father was amongst the first British troops into Jerusalem in 1918 under General Allenby, and I was amongst the last out in 1948. We stopped in the desert south of Bethlehem, and formed Brigade Square, probably the last time the British Army has done this. In the centre of the square we had four guns loaded with high-explosive (HE) shells, and laid on the nearest Jewish settlement, and one gun on each corner of the square laid over open sights and also loaded with HE shells. The next day, driving south, we passed the Egyptian Army moving north to invade Palestine. Their Army consisted solely of six artillery regiments with no infantry. They then ran out of 25-pounder ammunition and the invasion ground to a halt. This, of course, resulted in the formation of the state of Israel. We drove south for two days through the desert and finally crossed the Suez Canal at El Kantara and into Egypt.

48 Field Regiment then left Egypt and went to Benghazi in Cyrenaica. After eight months as a gunner subaltern I asked my commanding officer if he would recommend me for an Air OP course. He flatly refused, saying I did not know enough gunnery and that I lacked experience as a gunner officer!

After three years overseas I was to return to the UK by troopship, but at the last moment I was told that I had to take 100 German ex-prisoners of war back to Germany. After the war they did not wish to go back to a devastated Germany and so took contracts to work for the British Army as drivers, cooks and in other sundry jobs, and they continued to live in the old prisoner of war camp. On completion of their contracts they had to be sent back to Germany on leave. So I went to the camp to collect them. They were paraded in three ranks by an ex-regimental sergeant-major (RSM), who saluted me and reported them to be all present and correct. He then detailed one man to look after my baggage and another to be my batman. We then embarked on a Royal Naval destroyer and set sail from Benghazi for northern Italy. I had been given an enormous bundle of contracts and was told to get as many of the Germans as I could to sign new contracts to return, after leave, to Benghazi. I managed to get about two-thirds to sign. The rest of them lived in East Germany and knew that the Russians would not allow them to come back again.

On arrival in Trieste we were put into two railway carriages, which were then attached to various trains, and we started to wend our way through a devastated Europe. We first stopped at Villach, a British transit camp in Austria, where we got a meal, the last real food we were to get for another three days. I had no control over our destiny as the carriages would suddenly be hitched to a train and later decoupled and left in sidings miles from anywhere. We did stop at a station in the US zone and I managed to get hold of a rail transport officer and ask for food. He had none, but said he would arrange for some further down the line. This he did, and when we got there we got some ersatz coffee and a thin vegetable soup from a United Nations (UN) refugee kitchen. I had been told that our destination was Münster, but I was unaware that there were two towns of that name in Germany and that we had been routed to the wrong one. Finally, in the middle of the night, we were shunted into a siding. I found a displaced persons camp nearby and ordered the German commandant to feed and house my men. This was the first real food we had had for nearly three days.

I then found a British Kreis (district) resident officer who was running that part of Germany. He gave me an army truck and I drove a hundred and fifty miles north to Hamburg to find the nearest British troops. I went to the local Area Headquarters, got a British paymaster to go back to the camp and pay the men the money they were owed, and then managed to hand over all the documents. I was still dressed in khaki shirts and shorts at the time and it took some convincing to make the area commander believe that I was in fact who I said I was. I then drove back to the displaced persons camp to find that the Germans had all left, except the RSM. He said that as soon as they were paid they took off to find their homes, and he then said that he was leaving in about half an hour. So, my task completed, I set off again for Hamburg, where I spent a month's leave with my parents. My father was then with the Allied Military Government of Occupied Territories, more commonly known as Ancient Military Gentleman On Tour.

Whilst on leave in the UK, I visited the gunner postings branch in the War Office, to be told that I was to join a Gunner Parachute Regiment, about which I was very pleased. But just before I left I asked the staff captain what the chances were of an Air OP course. He asked me to wait and then said that yes, there was a vacancy on the next course and would I like to go. I said that yes, I certainly would. I would have to pass the RAF medical and aptitude tests, which I had already done, but I still had to go to Biggin Hill and take them again, and of course I managed to pass. So, in September 1949, I found myself at 21 Elementary Flying Training School at

RAF Booker, near High Wycombe, learning to fly a Tiger Moth biplane as an army officer under a RAF instructor, on exactly the same course that I should have been doing back in May 1944.

2
Learning to fly

RAF Booker, near High Wycombe, was a fairly small grass airfield and all the instruction and living accommodation was in very old wooden huts. I soon discovered that that the great majority of our time was spent in the classroom learning various different subjects such as the theory of flight, navigation, meteorology, airmanship, engines and many others. We had to take endless written examinations in these subjects, and a failure in any one would immediately result in us being returned to our units. We started flying after about two days and usually managed up to two flights a day. Six of us started the course, five Royal Artillery lieutenants and one student from Transjordan. One British student left after a few days when it was discovered that, first of all, he was subject to air-sickness and, even more importantly, he was quite incapable of judging the height of the aircraft from the ground.

I started flying on the de Havilland Tiger Moth, a two-seater fabric-covered biplane. My instructor was a flight lieutenant in the RAF. Over the next fortnight,

The de Havilland Tiger Moth

22 Learning to fly

I did about eighteen flights with my instructor in the front seat and myself behind. I was quickly taught spinning and how to recover from a stall, and practised taking off and landing into wind. After ten hours and forty minutes' instruction my instructor, after a fairly good take-off and landing on my part, said that I could go off on my first solo flight, and got out of the aircraft. I took off and climbed and turned crosswind and then on to the downwind leg when I suddenly realised that I was on my own. It was one of the greatest experiences of my life and I was extremely euphoric after realising that I was at last flying the aircraft on my own. However, I soon realised that I now had to land the aircraft, which was going to be far more difficult. However, I did manage to carry out a reasonably good landing.

For the next week I did both dual and solo flying, and perfected much of what I had already learned. In addition, I was taught how to restart the engine in flight, side-slipping and steep turns, and also using the engine on the approach to landing; a technique that I was later to use on the Auster, as it facilitated very short landings and take-offs from small strips. I then managed to pass the twenty-hour test.

Throughout this time, of course, we continued with learning ground subjects in the classroom. We were studying one day – a very boring talk on meteorology – when there was a loud bang and a lot of noise on the roof of the wooden hut. We rushed out and found that the hut was covered in small branches and twigs which had come from a line of trees, just behind the hut. It was quite obvious that an aircraft had flown into the trees. It was in fact a student from the previous course who had misjudged his height and ploughed a Tiger Moth through the top the trees. He did, however, manage to keep the aircraft flying. Despite losing about eight inches of his propeller, he completed a circuit and landed the aircraft in more or less one piece, much to his and everybody else's surprise.

For the next fourteen days, it was very much the same, except that I did begin to learn how to fly on instruments. I did a certain amount of training on the Link Trainer in the hangar. The Link Trainer was I suppose the forerunner of the modern flight simulator. It was basically a box in which you sat in darkness, being able to see only the flying instruments. It did move about in three directions and generally made you totally confused and taught you to rely on the instruments rather than your own senses. But it did teach you the basic way to fly an aircraft blind, relying totally on instruments.

One day, having taxied out on to the airfield, I was told by my instructor to put a large canvas cover over my cockpit, so that I could see nothing but the instruments, and then he told me to take off. I took off on instruments and, as I thought, steadily climbed away and levelled out, at which stage he told me to pull back the canopy and I found that I had flown through 90° and was heading straight down back into the ground: a very chastening experience. I also did a lot of precautionary landings and practised forced landings into what one hoped were suitable fields, and also a

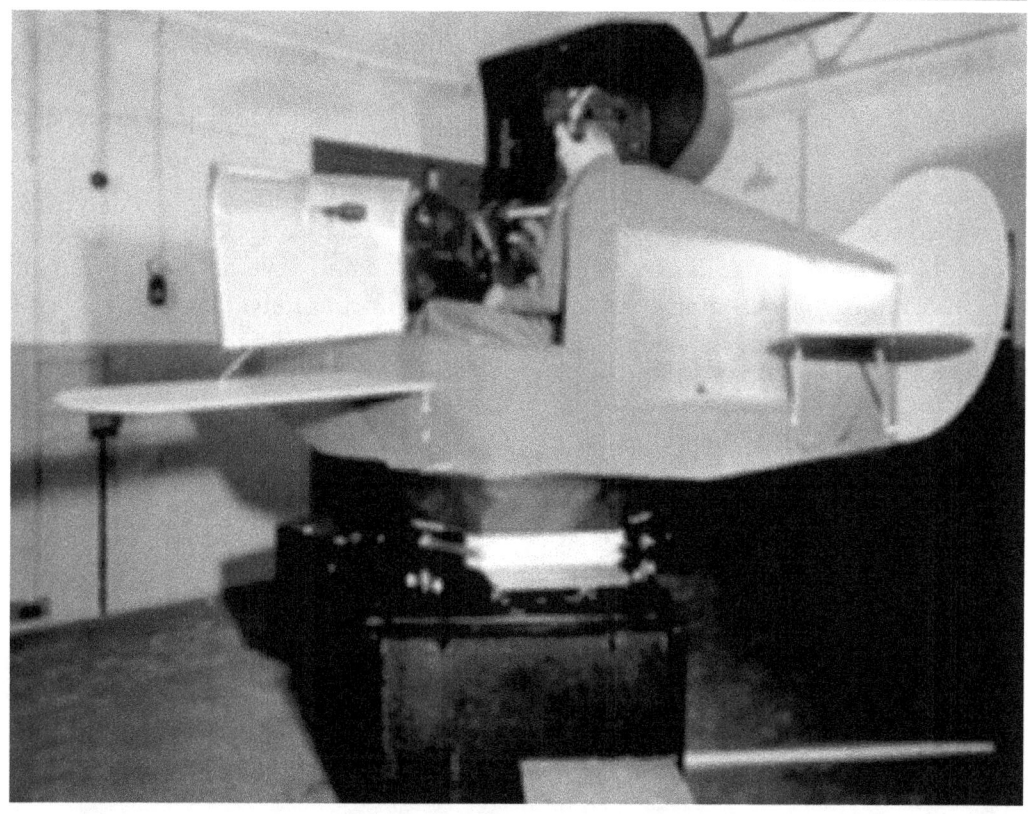

The Link Trainer in the hangar at Booker

certain amount of map reading when we flew to another airfield and back again. One day, with my instructor on the Tiger Moth, we were to practise low flying at about fifty feet. He was flying the aircraft across a fairly small field when there was a loud bang and the aircraft was thrown up into the air. Nothing was said, and he climbed away to a safe height and levelled off. He finally said to me "Could I see the wheels from the rear cockpit?" I had a look and said that I couldn't, but that I had seen a blue flash in the corner of the field, which was probably from a broken power cable. He did not reply, but flew straight back to the airfield and landed in an obscure far corner of it, whereupon he got out had a look at the wheels and the landing gear and couldn't find anything wrong, so he then quietly taxied back as far away from the control tower as he could and parked the aircraft. Nothing further was said of this incident! We were extremely lucky, of course, in that the bottom half of the wheels had hit a high-powered cable and thrown the aircraft upwards. A friend of mine, on another course, had a similar experience with not quite so much luck. His aircraft went straight in and he woke up in front of roaring flames and quite convinced himself that he was in Hades. However, it turned out that both he and the instructor were lying down in a farmhouse kitchen in front of

24   Learning to fly

a large log fire, having been rescued by the farmer. They both survived, and he did in fact get his wings.

Most of December and January was spent on the Tiger Moth practising and improving our flying techniques. I also had my first flight in an Auster with an instructor, but it wasn't until early January 1950 that I did my first solo on the Auster Mark V. At this time I was taught aerobatics on the Tiger Moth and learnt to do stall turns, rolls, rolls off the top, loop the loop and inverted spinning. This was enormous fun, although very demanding. Unfortunately, this was the last I did because the Auster was not cleared for aerobatics; it seems the wings can fall off. I also completed night flying in the Tiger Moth.

The Auster Mark VI

Towards the end of January I should have done a dual cross-country flight, but my instructor forgot and I was sent on a solo cross-country flight in an Auster. I had to fly to Marlborough, turn left and then on to Middle Wallop in Hampshire, land, have lunch and return direct to Booker. However, in spite of my meticulous preparation in navigation for the trip, I did not find my first two waypoints or even Marlborough. However, I turned left and set course for Middle Wallop, which again I did not find, and suddenly found myself over an airfield with a large hangar on which was the word "Southampton". At this stage knowing where I was, I abandoned air navigation and map-read my way back to Middle Wallop for a rather late lunch. I then set off back to Booker but, as before, I missed the first two waypoints. At this stage I again abandoned aerial navigation and took to low flying, found the nearest railway station, read the name and map-read my way back to Booker. There was much muttering in the corridors of power and I expected that I would be returned to my unit. However, the next day, another student on the same course took the same aircraft also on a cross-country. He too got hopelessly lost in bad weather and had to force land on the Vickers airfield in the middle of the London Control Zone, where no other aircraft was flying due to the bad weather. After this the instructors decided to have a closer look at the aircraft and in fact found that the compass had a 10° error in it, and so luckily we were both exonerated.

On 21 February, I took my final tests on the Auster, which I managed to pass, and was then passed out of the Elementary Flying Training School, and went on to the 227 Air OP Operational Conversion Unit at Middle Wallop. This part of the course was to learn to fly the Auster V and VI and to learn the flying skills and techniques required, but also to learn to control the fire of artillery from the air, which was the basic skill required of any Air OP pilot. Apart from the chief flying instructor, all the instructors were captains in the Royal Artillery.

Virtually all flying from then on was to be done at a low level, 50 to 500 feet, and operating from small grass strips of 300 by 6 yards. We did not, therefore, carry parachutes. This meant that all landings had to be on three points and engine assisted, which was fundamentally different from my previous RAF training.

I was immediately checked out on the Auster V and flew solo the next day, and for the next month flying was half dual and half solo, mainly practising short landings on to forty various fields all over Hampshire. Some of these were extremely small. One I remembered could only be approached uphill, regardless of the wind. It had a 40° gradient and was only about 80 yards long. Take-off, of course, was then downhill. The Middle Wallop airfield was grass, but there was a tarmac perimeter track. Strips were marked out on it in white paint 100 yards long and 6 yards wide. We had to learn to land within the white lines with up to a 45° crosswind. Once you learnt the technique, it was not too difficult. However, the Jordanian student pilot was rather over-keen and he landed with the brakes full on. The result was that the aircraft ended up on its back with him hanging upside-down from his straps. Only his pride was hurt.

This training continued throughout April and May, with the addition of many low-level cross-country exercises. We also learnt to conceal our approach to landing on a strip by flying in from a mile away at about 150 to 200 feet straight over the strip and then go on for a mile, complete a square circuit, and about a mile before the strip drop down to about 30 feet and land straight on. Similarly, on take-off, as soon as you were airborne you flew for a mile at about 30 to 40 feet before climbing away. This was very necessary because on operations our strips would often be less than a mile behind the front line, and therefore subject to enemy artillery fire if they knew where we were. We learnt to drop messages on to our ground crew with

26 Learning to fly

a small pouch with two streamers on it, and also to pick up messages. The ground crew erected two masts about 20 feet apart and 20 feet high with a loop of cord hanging from the top with the message bag on the bottom. The pilot then flew in at about 40 feet and trailed a four-pronged fork on a long line beneath the aircraft, which caught the top of the cord and, if lucky, you flew away with the message. Very Heath Robinson, but it actually worked.

Towards the end of the course we did many sorties on the artillery ranges at Larkhill on Salisbury Plain, practising our ability to control artillery from the air, which was of course the basic reason for our existence. Fourteen days before the end of the course I was doing this on the Larkhill ranges. I did a shoot in the morning, and after lunch took off to do another shoot. Coming into land on the grass, I felt I was flying too fast and reduced my air speed, with the result that I stalled and crashed the aircraft, narrowly missing a truck which was full of cans of aviation fuel. It subsequently transpired that the instructor had not noticed during lunch that the wind had gone round through 180° and had not therefore changed the landing T so that I was in fact landing downwind. It was ruled that it was his fault and I was once again exonerated.

Nearly the end of my flying career

I finished the Air OP course, with 169 flying hours, on 21 June 1950, and was awarded my wings. I was then posted, after some leave, to 656 Air OP Squadron in Malaya.

3
Flying in Hong Kong and on to Korea

In August 1950 I spent three weeks on a troopship to Singapore, and joined 656 Air OP Squadron in Malaya early in September. The squadron was then operating all over Malaya, in support of the Army against the Chinese Communist terrorists, and were flying more hours in a year than the whole of the Far East Air Force. I was then posted to 1907 Flight in Seremban in south Malaya. I started flying with them and had just about completed my familiarisation with flying over the jungle when I was summarily posted to Hong Kong to join 1903 Independent Air OP Flight in Hong Kong. After another week at sea I arrived in Hong Kong and started flying again in late September as a section pilot in 1903 Flight.

1903 was an independent flight with five aircraft and six pilots (four captains and two subalterns). One was the officer commanding (OC) and five were section pilots. The ground crew numbered about fifty, half RAF aircraft technicians and half Royal Artillery drivers and signallers. Each section was autonomous and

Hong Kong in 1950. Cricket Club to right of Hong Kong and Shanghai Bank

capable of operating independently in the field. There was one pilot, one RAF airframe mechanic and one RAF engine mechanic, plus a gunner driver/signaller with a 3-ton truck and a gunner driver/batman with a jeep. The flight was based on a small 300-yard-long strip in paddy fields in the New Territories at Pak Yuan in Hong Kong, a few miles south of the Chinese border. We were housed in two old Chinese buildings.

Mao Zedong, having triumphed over his nationalist opponents in the civil war, had declared the People's Republic of China the previous year, and the threat to the Colony was considered very real. The Army had the best part of an Army Corps stationed in the Colony and was at fifty per cent readiness at all times. This meant that all units had to have half their forward positions on the frontier manned day and night.

We had some routine tasks such as dropping rations and ammunition to the forward units in difficult locations. This was done by taking off the left-hand door of the aircraft and dropping sandbags packed with the necessary supplies on to the forward infantry. We also did a regular reconnaissance of the Chinese frontier in order to detect any Chinese build-up which might constitute a direct threat to the Colony. We carried out a regular oblique photo-reconnaissance of the whole frontier, including the coastline of Mirs Bay, but we were not allowed to cross the Chinese frontier. As we had a small photographic unit in the flight we were able to do our own processing. The RAF had a reconnaissance Spitfire equipped with cameras, which flew well into China at over 30,000 feet, at which height the Chinese, even if they saw it, could not shoot it down.

We sometimes used the main airfield at RAF Kai Tak and also an RAF fighter strip at Sek Kong in the New Territories. The longer fairways on the Fanling golf club were very good for short-landing practice, though this was not too popular with the local golfers. There was also a long sandy beach on the south of Lantau Island, then virtually uninhabited but now a modern city and a major airport. We would land on the wet sand at low tide, have a swim and then lift up the tail of the aircraft and turn it round to take off. There were only two places to land on Hong Kong Island. One was the racecourse in Happy Valley. The other was the cricket club, which was quite tricky as it was surrounded by very tall buildings.

A fair amount of our time was spent on practising control of artillery fire on the Castle Peak range, a small mountainous area to the west of the Colony. This was good training both for us and for the resident gunner regiments, and stood us in good stead later on in Korea. We flew regular sorties to clear Castle Peak of people before the artillery could start firing. The Chinese would sometimes put grandma out onto the range the night before and hope to collect a very large monetary compensation if later she was shelled.

Flying in Hong Kong and on to Korea

We had good liaison with the Royal Navy and carried out deck landings on an aircraft carrier out in Mirs Bay. Being the junior pilot I was sent on board with a wireless set in order to speak to the pilots. This proved quite useless in that the small Army set (a British Army Wireless Set No. 62 MKII) was completely drowned out by the powerful Navy sets. The first Auster made a perfect landing right on the aft deck, in those days without the benefit of an arresting hook. The ship was steaming into a strong wind and a fairly lumpy sea, so there was about a 30- to 35-knot wind over the deck. The Auster was landing at about 40 to 45 knots, so it virtually stopped dead in a few yards. The pilot, not knowing what do, taxied forward and stopped alongside the Island, the control centre of the carrier, halfway down the flight deck on the starboard side, whereupon the Navy flashed a green light at him, expecting him to go back to the aft end of the carrier and take off from there. He didn't fancy turning round on the flight deck in the wind in case he was blown off the ship, so he stood on the brakes, put on full throttle, and took off. Needless to say he was airborne in a few yards but he held the aircraft down on the deck until he disappeared off the front end of the carrier and then climbed steeply away. This caused great consternation to the Navy who sounded all the alarms on board, thinking that they had an aircraft in the drink. We were a little unpopular as a result with our naval friends for some time afterwards.

We also practised spotting for naval frigates firing at a small uninhabited island in Tolo Harbour in the north of the Colony. This proved to be quite a challenge as the naval guns were very high velocity, and consequently had a very flat trajectory, which meant that if you missed the target the shell was likely to go on for a considerable way. I was spotting one day for a small frigate, but failed to see the first ranging round so I ordered a major correction of about 1,000 yards, which I did not see so either. So, in desperation, I ordered yet another big correction. This time I did see the burst, but unfortunately it was on the mainland, luckily in an uninhabited part of the Colony, so no one was any the wiser! However, this was all good experience and we became much better at it in the future.

Sometime later we left the strip at Pak Yuan for Sek Kong and set up on the end of the RAF airfield north of Lion Rock. The runway was covered with pressed steel plate, which did not flood but made for quite bumpy landings. The RAF had a squadron of twin-boomed Vampire jets based here, so we had to fit in with their flying programme, which was not entirely satisfactory. However, they did give us the opportunity to practise fighter evasion with them. An Auster would take on two Vampire jets armed with cameras rather than guns. They attempted to shoot us with their cameras, whilst we did our best to evade them. In fact it was far easier than expected, provided you could get a sight of the aircraft before they saw you. When they attacked you slowed down and went into a steep diving turn in towards the Vampire, and then got down as low as possible into the hills. The combination of the jets' fast speed and the slow speed of the Auster meant that the jets invariably overshot. In fact, the Vampires never got a confirmed kill on us over very many practice dogfights. This gave us some confidence.

Eventually a permanent strip was built for us at the head of Shatin Bay, a long inlet running north to south from Tolo Harbour. It was a 300-yard tarmac strip and even had a small control tower. The flight was housed in an old Chinese hotel about a mile north of the strip on the side of the inlet. The officers' mess was another mile further on, again in a small hotel with its own little jetty, so we were able to keep a dinghy and a small yacht. We were all bachelors and lived a fairly hectic life. I raced in a Dragon yacht with an Olympic helm at the Royal Hong Kong Yacht Club on Kellett Island in the harbour, and was also a member of the Hong Kong Club and the Hong Kong Cricket Club. At weekends, we would move to one of the bank messes on the island and the bankers would often take over our mess for a country weekend. One afternoon, after a heavy curry lunch, one of the pilots set off single-handedly in the jointly owned yacht. He had still not returned by early evening, so we had to scramble an aircraft go and look for him. He was found at anchor in a small inlet fast asleep, much to his great embarrassment. Another day, flying over a small uninhabited island we spotted a large abandoned motor launch, which we managed to recover. It was in fact an RAF launch, which had been sold at auction to a Chinese gentleman. With the help of the Air Sea Rescue Unit at RAF Kai Tak, we managed to make it seaworthy, so the flight ended up with a splendid launch, which was great for water-skiing and picnicking.

This rather idyllic existence was brought to a sudden and abrupt end on 28 June 1951, when we were given ten days' notice to set sail for Korea. It was a frantic rush to get the whole unit onto a war footing. I was acting as the flight quartermaster at the time, and was given free rein in the Ordnance Depot. I managed to change all our wireless sets and batteries for brand new ones and also changed a number of vehicles and much other kit to bring us up to War Establishment. On 7 July we flew the aircraft from Shatin to Kai Tak and the whole flight and vehicles drove to the docks. Everything was then lightered out to the carrier HMS Unicorn, which was lying in Hong Kong harbour. The next day we sailed for Japan. The Royal Navy

 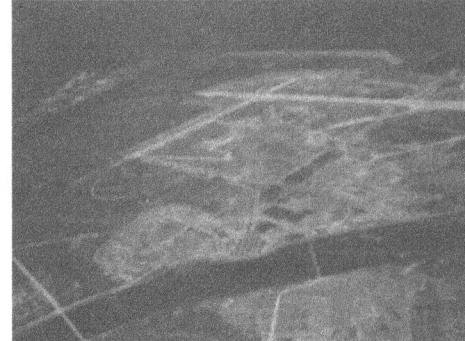

Left: Hiroshima; right: Iwakuni airfield

The Dome: Ground Zero of the Atomic Bomb on Hiroshima

refuelled our aircraft and vehicles and looked after us extremely well, in spite of the fact they were unable to fly their own aircraft because we were occupying the flight deck. We arrived at Iwakuni on the Inland Sea of Japan on 14 July. We had hoped to fly off the carrier, but the captain would not allow it as the ship was in a mined channel and he would not have been able to rescue us if anyone fell into the drink. So once again the whole flight was lightered ashore to the American and Royal Australian Air Force Base at Iwakuni. We spent about four days flight testing the aircraft and generally sorting ourselves out. During this time I flew over the Inland Sea and the beautiful island of Mia Jima and also over Hiroshima, which was still radiating, and took a photograph of the Dome from 100 feet.

One day, we took a couple of jeeps and drove up into the mountains to see the countryside. Japan was then still a feudal country, and of course it was still being governed by General Douglas MacArthur. We came to a small inn and asked whether they could give us lunch. Before we knew what had hit us, we were all divested of our uniforms and plunged into hot baths followed by cold baths, and were scrubbed down by half a dozen girls. They then gave us a very good lunch sitting on the floor and afterwards our jungle green uniforms, which had been laundered and starched, were returned to us. Quite a change from Hong Kong.

On 27 July we loaded the five aircraft with spares, which we tucked into every nook and cranny in the fuselage. We each took an RAF technician in the back seat. We were grossly overloaded, but knew that all the take-offs from then on would be from American airfields with long runways. We left Iwakuni and flew to the South Island, where we landed at an American airfield at Ashyia, refuelled and took off again, and formed up in flight formation heading over the sea towards Pusan on the southern tip of Korea, 140 miles away, which was just within the Auster's range, provided that they was no strong headwind! We married up with a Sunderland flying boat from the RAF squadron at Iwakuni above the airfield, but had no radio contact with him. He would then fly ahead of us and we would set our compasses to follow his track. He would then disappear for about ten to

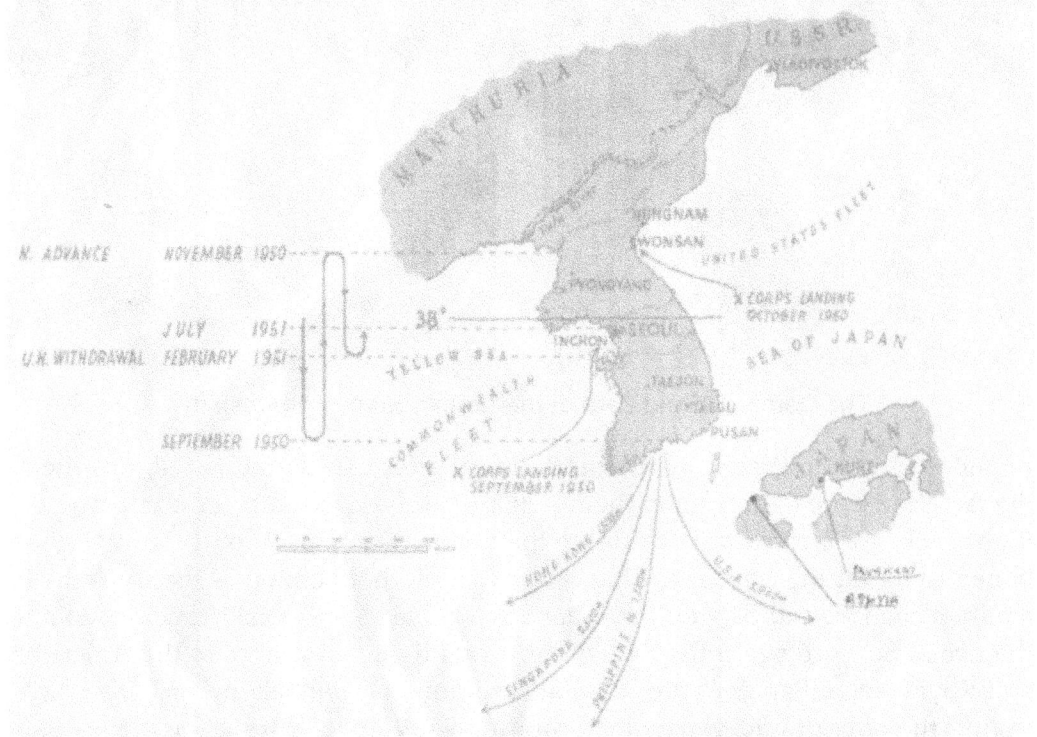

Route from Iwakuni via Ashyia and Pusan to the 38th parallel

fifteen minutes, and would then reappear in front of us, so that we could reset our compasses. We successfully arrived in Pusan and landed at K9, an American airfield. After landing, we found that we had broken three tail wheels because we were so grossly overloaded. The solid rubber tail wheel was attached to a steel bar which was pivoted, and the other end was attached by a rubber band about an inch thick to the stern post of the aircraft; extremely basic, but it did actually work. We spent the next day there, and then on 29 July took off again for Taegu K2, an American fighter strip, where we refuelled and replaced another three tail rubber bungees and flew off again for Anson K6, yet another American airfield, where we refuelled and again replaced a couple of tail wheel bungees before setting off for Seoul City airport K16. On 30 July we flew from Seoul to the Eighth Army light aircraft strip, which was based on the old racecourse just outside Seoul.

On 31 July I flew to Inchon on the west coast and then on to the Imjin River on the 38th parallel and reconnoitred the new strip which the sappers had prepared for us with the Commonwealth Division, which had only formed about a week before. Then back to Seoul. On 1 August we flew to our first strip. This was a 300-yard dirt strip alongside the deserted village of Tokchong beside a small river. We dispersed the aircraft between the thatched huts and concealed them with camouflage nets. These were mud-walled huts with thatched roofs, and surprisingly with central

Flying from Pusan to Seoul

heating. There was a charcoal fire outside the hut and the flue ran underneath the mud floor and out the other side. We didn't occupy these huts because they were plagued with rats, which were carrying the bubonic plague. Over the next two days I carried out my first two operational sorties and also directed my first shoot with airburst shells against a Chinese infantry section which was dug in.

When we flew from Iwakuni we left one pilot and the rest of the flight and vehicles behind. They then drove to a Japanese port and sailed to Pusan, where they got another ship and sailed up the west coast, where the whole flight disembarked at Inchon and drove the fifty-odd miles from Inchon to join the flight on its new strip.

We had broken more tail wheels on the way up and on arrival. In effect, we had one aircraft operationally grounded because we had no more spares. However, our enterprising flight sergeant got hold of one of the main wheel rubber bungees, which were much, much larger, tied a knot in it and managed to fit it on to a tail wheel, so we remained airborne until we finally had spares flown up from Singapore.

34 Flying in Hong Kong and on to Korea

Tokchong strip: the aircraft can be seen between the huts and the camouflage nets

4
Joining the First Commonwealth Division

The 27 Infantry Brigade from Hong Kong arrived in Korea on 25 August 1950 and then, with the addition of the 3 Royal Australian Regiment became the 27 Commonwealth Brigade. The British 29 Infantry Brigade arrived on 3 November. These two brigades operated independently under American command until they joined the Commonwealth Division in July 1951.

On 28 July 1951, the 1st Commonwealth Division was formed at Tockchong, south of the Imjin River on the 38th parallel. This was a unique formation comprising basically the British 29th Infantry Brigade, the 27th Commonwealth Brigade and the 25 Canadian Brigade, 8th Royal Irish Hussars, and a Canadian squadron of Lord Strathcona's Horse and 45 Field Regiment RA, 16 Royal New Zealand Artillery Regiment and 2nd Royal Canadian Horse Artillery Regiment and also many other units from the Commonwealth. 1903 Flight joined four days later.

A US Harvard T6 Mosquito on Fort George strip

36 Joining the First Commonwealth Division

Daily maintenance

Captain Bob Begbie, a qualified Air OP pilot, was at this time with the 11 Sphinx LAA Battery, but he managed to get transferred to the Americans and flew with them as an Air OP pilot in Harvards, more commonly known as Mosquitos. He operated mainly with the 29 British Brigade and was awarded a US Air Medal. Unfortunately, he was unable to join the flight, as we already had a full complement of pilots.

The division covered about fifteen miles of the front and was dug in on a line of hills just south of the Imjin River, and included the former position of the famous Gloucestershire's Battle of the Imjin River, which took place a few months earlier. The Chinese 24th Army of three divisions was established about five to eight miles north of the Imjin River, so there was a large amount of no man's land between us, which the division started aggressively to patrol, up to company level, in order to dominate the ground. In early August, Operation Hunter followed by Operation Dirk took place. These were battalion-strength raids north of the Imjin River. This was followed by Operation Claymore, when the Canadian brigade crossed the river and attacked a Chinese position and then withdrew two days later. The flight was heavily involved in supporting all these operations, mainly in reconnaissance of the battlefield, opportunity shoots and providing defensive fire to the patrols, but also taking up company and battalion commanders to reconnoitre the positions which they were about to attack. During this time we engaged quite a

1903 AOP Flight September 1951: pilots in front row from left, Derek Jarvis, Terry Fitzgibbon, Dick Corfield, Ronnie Gower, Leslie Addington, Arthur Stewart-Cox

large number of opportunity targets and hostile batteries. On another day I caught a large number of Chinese infantry in the open and engaged them with an "Uncle Target", that is the three field regiments, a total of seventy-two guns.

Whilst working in support of Operation Claymore I had taken up my engine mechanic as an observer. Halfway into the sortie he tapped me on the shoulder and shouted at me and said that there were a lot of atmospherics. I removed my headset and realised of course of that it was medium machine-gun fire. I took swift evading action and in fact the aircraft was hit with a hole in the port flap, but no other damage. Afterwards he told me that it had been going on for some time, but he didn't want to interrupt me! We also did a certain amount of supply dropping of rations and ammunition to the patrols. At one stage we had to spray DDT and disinfectant on positions which had been occupied by other units and which our units were about to take over. Hygiene seemed not to be a strong point in other armies.

During this period Captain Leslie Addington found an enemy gun position which was out of range of our artillery, so he called in a US airstrike of four F84 Thunder Jets. They arrived and attacked the target and reported to the US liaison officer at Divisional Headquarters that the target was completely destroyed and that four guns were seen flying in the air! He reported at the same time, on another net, that the strike was not even in the same county, and so he ordered another strike. The same thing happened again: the target was not hit, so he called in a third strike and this time he flew directly over the target until the jets arrived above him. He then put the Auster into a steep dive down on to the enemy gun position, opened the window and fired red Very lights at the Chinese. This time the target was hit, but he then found himself at a very low height, three miles north of his own lines, and had a very uncomfortable flight home. He was awarded an immediate Distinguished Flying Cross.

Needless to say, the flight's flying hours were increasing, and in fact I did forty-five hours that month. The Tokchong strip was proving to be not entirely satisfactory. We had all dug in early on and I had dug a slit trench which accommodated my sleeping bag, covered by a two-man pup tent. During the night there was torrential rain and I woke up to find that my sleeping bag was completely awash, much to the amusement of the men in my section We learnt from this and never sited our strips too close to rivers in the future. I took off very early one morning, in what I thought was heavy mist, at about fifty feet, with the intention of climbing up through it and being on the front just after dawn. However, as soon as I was airborne I realised it was not mist but was very thick and heavy cloud, so I did a circuit at fifty feet and tried to land again. However, there was a large tree quite near to the approach to

A typical Korean village

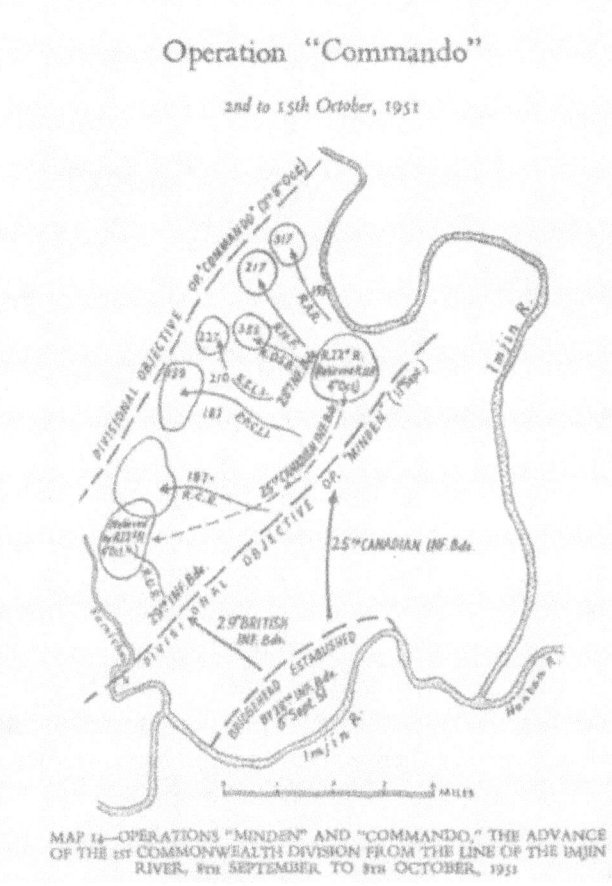

Operation Commando

the strip and I only narrowly avoided it and had to go round again.

We then moved a few miles north to a new strip which the Canadian engineers had prepared for us in a paddy field. The strip seemed fine on 11 September, but there was a torrential downpour that night and the next day the strip was at least a foot deep in mud and quite unusable. However, the Canadian sappers reacted very quickly and produced a 3-ton truck full of 45-gallon drums of napalm, which they poured all over the strip and then set alight. There was an enormous explosion, a fire and a great black cloud, but it worked. A few hours later, we all landed on to a hard baked surface.

At the end of September, the US 1st Corps with the 1st US Cavalry Division on the right, the Commonwealth Division in the centre and the 1st Republic of Korea Division on the left, were ordered to advance about 10,000 yards and to establish a new line on the high ground which the Chinese were then holding.

This was Operation Commando, which started on 2 October and ended successfully after much heavy fighting on 15 October. The battle opened with the artillery firing about 27,000 rounds, or 360 rounds per gun. The flight directed part of this barrage, particularly against enemy guns, which were heavily shelling our advancing infantry. Many US airstrikes were called in, including one night a B-29 Super Fortress. By 15 October, the division had secured all its objectives on the high ground, including the vital rocky feature known as point 355.

The flight was heavily involved throughout this time and kept two aircraft airborne over the front throughout the fourteen hours of daylight for eight days. This meant that at any one time two aircraft were on station, two were refuelling on the ground and one was on maintenance. One day, when taking off, an aircraft picked up a

Major Ronnie Gower receiving a "Mention In Dispatches" after Operation Commando

large stone which lopped about six inches off its wooden propeller. However, it managed to land safely. Within a few minutes another aircraft, which was running out of fuel, had landed. The ground crew managed to fit a new propeller, not an easy task, on to the first aircraft before the second one had been refuelled. In the first three days of the operation we found twenty active and thirty-eight possible enemy gun positions, many of which we immediately engaged. Throughout the operation we engaged a large number of opportunity targets on the retreating enemy and also in close support of our advancing infantry and against many hostile batteries. All this put a great strain on the pilots, but even more so on the aircraft and the ground crew.

The Divisional Headquarters then moved forward to a position just south of the bend in the Imjin River. The flight also moved to a new strip running northwest to southeast, virtually on the south bank of the river, which at this point ran through a gorge about 400 feet deep. Nearby was the main crossing point of the river, which was by a pontoon bridge. This was called Pintail and was on our main supply route. The only other crossing was a ford on the left of the front. Both these crossings were in great danger after heavy rains, when we had to fly upstream to report any dangerous rising water levels. No trouble in the winter; you could drive a Centurion tank over the ice. Later the Americans built a permanent bridge at Pintail.

Soon after we had dug in and consolidated these new positions, we had a visit from the Supreme Commander, General Matthew B. Ridgeway, and General Van Fleet, the Army commander. They were taken to a brigade OP near the front. The divisional commander said to General Ridgeway: "I would like to show you my artillery." The general said he would like that, so the divisional commander, Major-General Jim Cassels, known to us all as "Gentleman Jim", turned to the commander Royal Artillery, who had a remote headset on linked to a wireless set behind the hill, and said: "Willie, will you hit that hill over there." About 30 to 45 seconds later, 72 rounds from the divisional artillery landed on it. The supreme commander quite clearly thought that we had preregistered the target and that it was all a set-up, so he said: "Fine, but I would like to see you hit that hill over there", about 800 yards to the right. So they went through the same procedure and again about 45 seconds later, 72 rounds landed on that hill, to the clear amazement of the supremo. So much so that he turned to the divisional commander said: "I wish you to pass my congratulations to all the gunners in the Commonwealth Artillery", which was done.

The British way of controlling large concentrations of artillery dated back to 1939. One gun would be ranged onto a target at a particular map reference. Because of inaccurate maps and climate changes in temperature and weather conditions, the first round very rarely hits the target. When ranging is completed and a round has finally hit the target, that is its true position. During the ranging, every other command post in the divisional artillery copied the ranging corrections so that when it was decided to fire at the target all 72 guns were able to hit it simultaneously, delayed only by the time of flight of the shells. On the other hand, the American system was quite different. They had to range one gun from a single battery on to the target, but the other batteries could not follow suit. So therefore the other five or so batteries had also to range on to the same target consecutively. This took an inordinate amount of time. Anything from 20 to 30 minutes, by which time, of course the enemy had long since disappeared. A very pedestrian solution.

Korea "The Land of the morning calm" ... before the North Koreans and the Chinese destroyed it

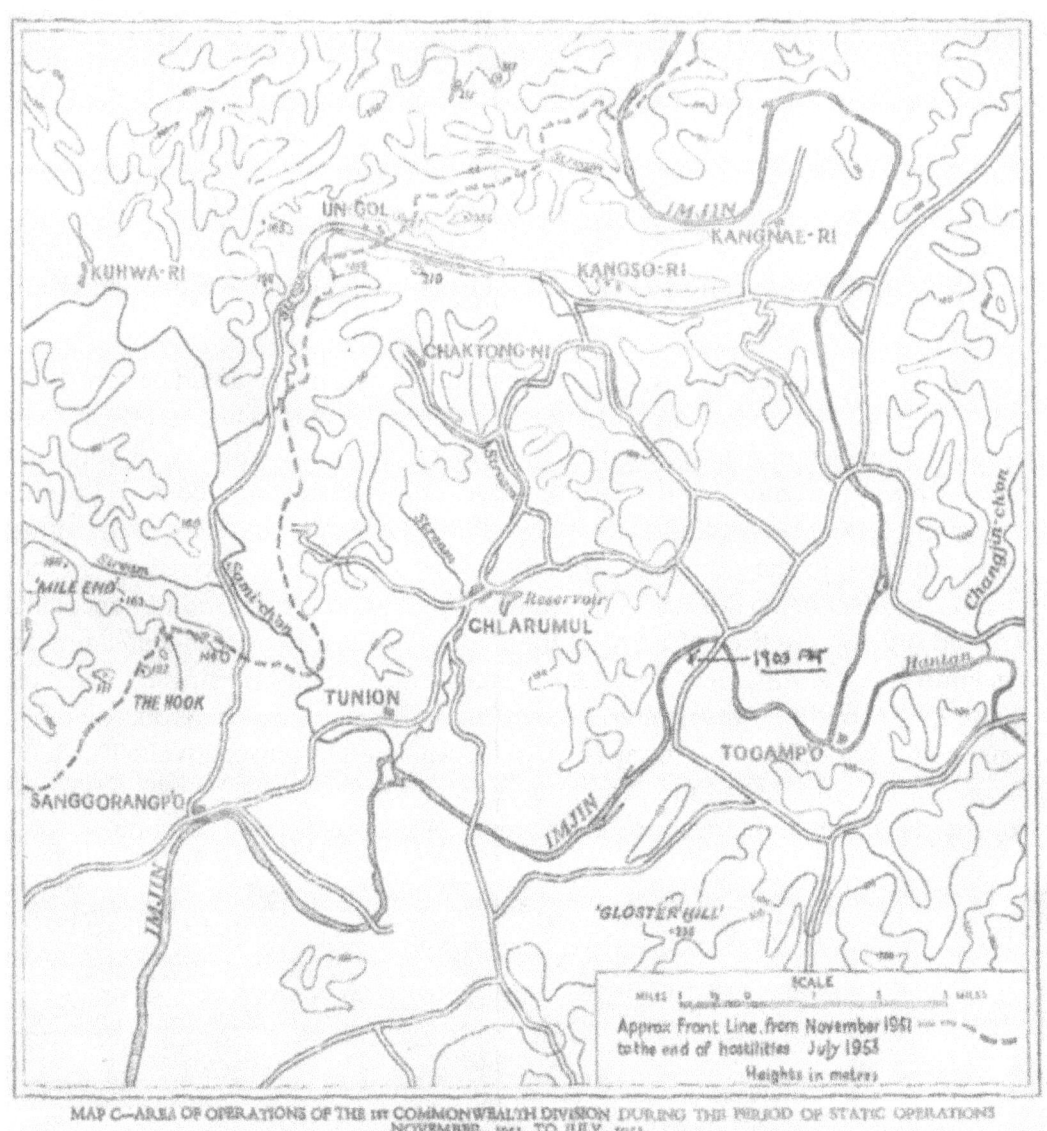

Approximate front line from November to July 1953

5

Into action and continuing operations up to December 1951

Within the first few weeks of arriving in Korea, we were forced to abandon the normal way of Air OP tactical flying. This was basically to fly at 50 feet behind hills on the front line, order a round and then climb up, spot the round and give a correction, and then get back down behind the hill. This was clearly not going to work so we soon began to fly higher, up to 2,000 feet over our own front lines where we were subject to quite heavy small arms fire. However, the real danger was from our own shells. There was so much artillery that it became almost impossible to find a piece of sky in which it was safe to fly. For instance, one day I was trying to destroy an enemy gun, using one gun from the "Persuaders", a US battery of four 8-inch guns. I was flying towards the target and looked up, only to see a 200-pound shell slowly passing above my canopy and going the same way. I had been careless and flown into its trajectory. Similarly, another pilot, again firing a "Persuader", flew into the trajectory of two shells which he had ordered. He was turned upside down and put into a spin, from which luckily, because he was very high, he managed to pull out of. So we were forced ever higher and further out over the front line, flying at 6,000 to 7,000 feet high and 3 miles beyond our own troops. There we were safe from our own shells and small arms fire, but had to contend with Chinese light anti-aircraft guns and sometimes even heavy anti-aircraft. On balance, this was by far the safer option.

After Operation Commando the war became fairly static, and the battle lines remained little changed until the end of the war. Both sides dug in deeply and it became very similar in some ways to World War I, with the massive use of artillery on both sides.

The flight got into a routine, carrying out the usual daily tasks over the enemy lines, and with the increasing number of large enemy attacks, we also put an aircraft on a daily dawn sortie. The pilot would take off about an hour before dawn, so as to be over the target at sunrise. Many sorties, particularly if there were enemy assaults, carried on after dark and the pilot only returned when he could no longer see targets or gun flashes. We improvised a flare path of five cigarette tins dug in on the left-hand side of the runway, so that when an aircraft was returning after dark the duty pilot would drive up the strip and put a splash of petrol into each can and on return set light to them. They lasted for five minutes, which was normally enough time because one could usually see the Imjin River in the moonlight.

The Chinese had a main supply route running south to Kuhwa-ri in their rear areas. This, we knew, was used to bring up reinforcements, supplies and ammunition at night. I was flying one evening when, just before dark, I noticed that this route was lined with small trees for about a thousand yards, which I had not noticed before. It was only when I realised that they were moving that it became apparent that it was a battalion of men, each carrying a small shrub, reminiscent of Shakespeare's Birnam Wood in *Macbeth*. Normally all daylight traffic stopped north of Kuhwa-ri, just out of range of our artillery, as the Chinese well knew, and they continued south after dark.

However, this time they had not realised that the new 8-inch battery could in fact just reach them. I fired two airborne burst rounds from each of the four 8-inch guns at the head of the column, and then moved the gunfire steadily up the column until I had covered the complete 1,000 yards. There was open paddy on either side of the road, so the infantry had nowhere else to go. It was a very satisfying shoot, which almost certainly resulted in one less battalion that we had to fight.

On another night sortie, I had a New Zealand gunner officer in the back seat. In the failing light I saw that the whole front was covered in heavy mist in all the valleys. It was only when I saw gun flashes through it that I realised it was not mist but gun smoke. The Chinese had launched two divisions with a heavy artillery barrage against one of our forward companies. I saw and reported twenty-nine active enemy gun positions, and I fired battery targets on two of them. By this time it was pitch dark and I had to return home.

The next day I went on R&R – rest and recuperation – more commonly known by the soldiers as I&I – intercourse and intoxication. We were allowed one R&R in a year's tour. The Australian pilot Captain Joe Luscombe also came with me, so we were flown down to Seoul airport and picked up a large four-engined US aircraft, which flew daily to Tokyo. As we landed, we were told to be back there in five days to the minute. The officers lived in the Maranouchi Hotel, the best in Tokyo. On arrival we were divested of our dirty combat uniforms and had an extremely welcome hot bath. Most of our time was spent on partying, although I did manage a round of golf on the only golf course in Japan at that time. One night we were both returning to our beds at about five o'clock in the morning when, to our amazement, we saw the divisional commander coming towards us in the corridor. We straightened up and said "Good morning, general". He stopped, looked us up and down, and said "Gentlemen, do you know it's a good morning?" and passed on his way.

After the leave, I did not return to the flight but flew down to Iwakuni, and on 27 November I air-tested a new aircraft, which had just been delivered. On the 29 I flew it to Ashyia. Because of the extremely bad weather I arranged for an RAF Sunderland to meet me over the airport, and we set off into the murk so that I could set my compass to follow him. The cloud base was well below 400 feet and it was raining very heavily with extremely bad visibility. The Sunderland met me again after about 10 minutes, but after that I never saw him again. Suddenly, to my left I saw land. This could only have been the island of Tsushima, which was way off my course to the west. I realised that the Sunderland pilot was taking me to another airfield far to the west of Pusan, which in fact was beyond my range, so I hastily had to re-plot my course, and with a degree of luck I did in fact manage to reach Pusan. Then I flew on to Taegu, then to Seoul, and thence to Fort George airstrip. I landed on all these American airfields and refuelled, but I did the whole trip in one day, something between four and five hundred miles. The next day, I did a normal reconnaissance flight over the front.

Our strip had now been named Fort George airstrip. We found that there was an enormous demand on us for providing liaison flights for senior officers, which took up a lot of flying hours, which we could ill afford. Consequently, a new flight was formed: 1913 Light Liaison Flight RAF, which joined us at Fort George. They had five Austers and the pilots were all ex-glider pilots: two officers and four sergeants. They relieved us of all liaison flying, and also took over some of the straightforward reconnaissance of the divisional front.

We found that we were getting a very large number of visiting senior officers who would usually arrive in the American Air OP aircraft – the L19 or Bird Dog. This was a metal-skinned aircraft with a slightly superior performance to that of the Auster, but its short landing ability was not as good. The American pilots found that 300 yards in which to land was somewhat of a challenge, and a number of them managed to crash.

So we had to build another cross strip 600 yards long running roughly north/south in order to accommodate them. Unfortunately, a US Marine Corsair

US Air OPs arrive on Fort George strip in L19s

46 Into action and continuing operations up to December 1951

Pontoon bridge at Pintail

which had been damaged over the front then crash-landed on the strip. Our RAF mechanics and the Americans managed eventually to put it together again, and he finally took off to fly back to his carrier.

The divisional commander, Major-General Jim Cassels, was well over six feet tall, and he found it inordinately difficult and uncomfortable to climb into the back seat of an Auster. So he asked the popular American Corps commander General "Mad" Mike O'Daniel if he would lend him an aeroplane. He, with typical American generosity, promptly gave him one, an L19. From then on he had his own personal aeroplane, which was flown by the second in command of 1913 Flight, complete with RAF markings. This did cause a certain amount of difficulty at the end of the war when they tried to hand it back to the RAF, who had of course never heard of it! I tended to be the personal pilot to the commander Royal Artillery, who was also the deputy divisional commander, and flew him very many times. About every three weeks he would fly with me over the front to see and test the artillery. He was a remarkably good gunner and from the back seat of an Auster, which is

Bofors LAA guns of 11 Sphinx Battery RA guarding Pintail Bridge. Six months earlier, this battery had engaged Chinese infantry over open sights during the Gloucester's Imjin battle about four miles to the west. Soon after this picture was taken they were converted to become a 4.2 inch Mortar Battery

US Army Beaver and US Marine Corps Corsair. Corporal Parr RAF telling the Americans how to repair it

extremely difficult to do, he would fire one or two divisional targets of seventy-two guns and never made a mistake.

By the end of November, the weather was becoming extremely cold, but with beautiful clear skies and occasionally heavy snowfalls. By this time, the whole flight were really well dug in and we had built showers fed by jerricans from above, used only in the summer. We had made heaters from used 25-pounder cartridge cases. A hole was drilled in the side and a copper tube inserted and about 4 inches of sand put in the bottom. The pipe was then drip fed from a jerrican full of aviation fuel and a chimney was made from the cartridge cases. Dangerous, as they were prone to blow up occasionally, but they were very effective. I also managed to barter from the Americans some space heaters. They were about 2 feet round and even had a sort of carburettor to control the flow. They were excellent, but again a fire hazard. We bartered with the Americans with gin and beer, as their troops were not allowed any alcohol. We got a small beer and alcohol allocation which came up with the rations. In this way, for a crate of gin, I managed to acquire a large American squad tent, which we used to make the flight cookhouse and the men's dining hall. It also included a large amount of fitted timber, so I had a big hole dug which we lined with wood on the floor and sides and made a table for six. Tents were put on the top to make a very comfortable, although small, officers'

Pilots' mess

Cookhouse area

mess. We even managed a white tablecloth, which we got out of the Ordnance Field Park. It was a burial shroud, complete with brass rings along the edges. We had an orphaned Korean boy called Kim, who was aged about sixteen. He ran the mess for us in return for accommodation, clothing and food. He would regularly go back to rear headquarters and to Seoul to collect our whisky ration and other goodies. Apparently he had an uncle in Seoul who ran a distillery, and one evening after supper he placed a bottle of brandy on the table and said "Me presento", with a great grin on his face, to the flight commander. It was a bottle neatly covered in cellophane with a smart label which read "Old Seoul Brandy, brewed from the finest botanicals". Once Kim had left, we judiciously opened the bottle and poured some of it on to the floor as though we had drunk it, as we did not wish to hurt his feelings. The next day, we got the medical officer to analyse it for us. It was made from neat wood alcohol coloured with urine! Very many US soldiers in Seoul died of this hooch. We were lucky indeed. Our troops also tried to brew their own hooch. Four signallers in the divisional headquarters collected some rotten apples from an orchard, which they put into a bucket with pure antifreeze taken from one of the vehicles. One evening, when it was nicely fermented they retired to their "hoochi" or dug-out, and drank the lot. The next day three of them were out line laying. The sergeant asked where the fourth was. They said they didn't know, but he was later found frozen stiff in his sleeping bag. A stern lesson to the rest.

The Korean climate had extremes of temperature, ranging from 100 in the summer to 40 degrees of frost in the winter. In the summer, we flew either in a lightweight tropical flying suit or just our underpants, and we were gently fried under a perspex canopy. The winter did present much greater problems. It was so cold, the ground was frozen to a depth of 2 feet, rather like tundra, so that you could not dig unless you used dynamite. If you touched vehicles or metal with your bare hands you lost the skin off your palms. At night, if you went out for a pee it tinkled before it hit the ground. No water was used in vehicle radiators, only pure antifreeze, and all vehicles had to be started up and moved every two hours

Into action and continuing operations up to December 1951

during the night to stop them freezing to the ground. We were equipped with a plastic sort of tent over the engine cowling with a Valor stove inside. It was utterly useless, as the paraffin froze up. It took five of us swinging the prop in turn trying to start the engine before dawn. You could get up enough oil pressure to fly, but it still took 30 minutes to an hour to get the engine to start. We did have leather fur-lined Irving flying suits, but they also proved to be inadequate and were simply discarded. We had the RAF wool-lined flying boots, very impressive, but again useless in the numbing cold with 40 degrees of frost on the ground and a further degree for every thousand feet. We were flying usually in about 46 degrees of frost. We ended up using the infantryman's boot, a size too large, with a nylon net mesh in the sole and two pairs of heavy woollen socks. The sweat went through the mesh, and formed a layer of ice in the sole the boot, giving another layer of insulation. It just prevented frostbite. We dressed in very heavy woollen drawers, with openings back and front, and a heavy string vest topped off with a normal vest, a thick khaki shirt and a heavyweight pullover and a string mesh sort of scarf. We then wore normal combat uniforms, which had four to five layers of a sort of nylon; they were very efficient. Then on top of that we wore an extremely large fur-lined parka with a tail which came through your legs and buttoned up on the front. We wore a leather flying helmet with a face mask and microphone with the parka hood on top. This came forward with a wire front so that you could adjust it to use binoculars. We then had pure silk gloves, which had six layers inside a heavy leather gauntlet. To cap it all off, we then wore a US back parachute from the head down to the back of your knees. This did help prevent the searing cold from the steel armour plate under the seat and back. All this did just stop us getting frostbite. On landing, my crew would push the aircraft under the camouflage net, take off the side door and lift me out in the sitting position, defrost the facemask and then spend 2 to 3 minutes gently pulling me up to a standing position so that I could then drive off in the jeep for a debriefing at flight headquarters, which was a 3-ton truck dug in under a camouflage net. It was little wonder that some of us, years later, ended up with skin cancer and bad backs.

There was a heavy fall of snow one night, so we got the sappers along with a bulldozer to clear a 6-foot-wide path down the centre of the runway. Unfortunately, it also left banks of snow on either side of the track. I managed to take off before dawn, with no problem, but there was a low cloud base that day and the aircraft iced up so I could not see out of the windscreen. I opened the window and took off my straps, leant forward and managed with my gauntlet to clear about 8 inches from the bottom left-hand corner of the windscreen. On landing, I had to lean forward to the left and look through this small gap, and on the first attempt I found myself landing on the piled snow on the left of the runway and had to go round again. The second time I came in from further out and lined the aircraft up and hoped for the best and managed to land safely on the 6-foot cleared runway between the banks of snow.

We had another difficulty with the cold weather: in one week three aircraft on dawn sorties failed to get off the 600-yard runway and all ended up with some degree of damage on the end of the runway. We suspected that it was due to hoarfrost, but were not quite sure. Knowing that an Auster had operated in the Antarctic on skis, we signalled the Air Ministry for a report of the expedition, but we never received a reply. When I next had to take off on a dawn sortie I noticed that the aircraft was heavily covered in what I again thought was hoarfrost, until I looked at it carefully and realised that the aircraft was completely covered in about an inch or two of solid clear ice, which obviously made the aircraft grossly overloaded and spoilt the aerofoil shape and would have meant a severe loss of lift. I sent one of my crew to the cookhouse and he came back with two blocks of cooking salt which we broke up into pieces and then wiped the whole of the aircraft with them. The ice completely fell off in a matter of minutes. I took off and we never had that problem again. This, however, did cause another problem during the next summer, but more of that later.

6

Continuing operations: from December 1951

The numbers of Chinese guns grew rapidly over this period. They had large numbers of both light and field artillery and also plenty of 122-mm medium and 152-mm heavy guns. Their guns soon outnumbered us by about four to one. However, our command and control of artillery was far superior to theirs and we managed to gain complete mastery over them. So much so that all their field artillery had to be deployed in single guns, each one being dug into a hillside from behind and fired from a small hole in the forward slope of the hill. This severely restricted their flexibility. We also forced their medium and heavy artillery to dig in, and they had to provide very heavy cover, sometimes concrete, over each gun.

We had no medium or heavy artillery of our own, which was a great disadvantage until the US 1st Corps allocated to us 936 Field Artillery Battalion, which consisted of eighteen 155-mm guns and a battery of four 8-inch guns known as the "Persuaders". These two units were virtually under our command, and remained with us for about a year. Initially we did have a certain amount of difficulty with 936 Battalion, because we were using different signals procedures and also different fire order procedures. This was appreciated, after a short time, by the Americans, so they asked us to teach them our methods and procedures as they thought that they were far better than their own! So we permanently attached to the battalion two New Zealand gunner/signallers; one sat in their Fire Direction Centre and reinterpreted our orders, and the other taught the American officers and command post staffs our signals procedures. We then lent them a pilot for a few days to teach the American gunner officers British fire order procedures. We also made similar arrangements with the "Persuaders". So we eventually ended up with an American medium regiment and a heavy battery completely integrated into the Commonwealth Artillery. Once these arrangements were bedded in, 936 Battalion became an extremely efficient unit and we used them in all our divisional targets and many other tasks.

When you ordered a divisional target, the Brigade Major Royal Artillery (BMRA), over the air, would allocate the three Commonwealth Field Regiments, and the American Medium Regiment and sometimes the 61st Light Regiment of 4.2-inch mortars. Then, when each unit was ready, they reported so to the pilot. There was always great competition to see which unit would be ready to fire first. One day, the British unit was first, the New Zealand second, and the American third, followed

52 Continuing operations: from December 1951

by the Royal Canadian Horse Artillery Regiment, to their great chagrin and hurt pride. One day in Japan, I met an officer whom I knew from the 936 Battalion, and was surprised to see him wearing a "1 Comwel" badge on his uniform instead of the US 1st Corps badge. I asked him why he was wearing it, and he said: "Gee, we're a member of the Commonwealth!" I had no answer to this.

At one stage the 3rd US Division had moved in on our right, and the Commander Royal Artillery (CRA) asked me to fly him across to visit them. The weather was extremely bad with a 200-foot cloud base. However, we set off into the more mountainous country on our right flank and it started to snow quite heavily. I found myself flying up a valley in decreasing visibility with the aircraft beginning to ice up. I then realised that I could not climb out of it at the far end, so I was forced to do an extremely tight turn and go back the way I had come. Luckily we made it back to the strip in a snowstorm, and I had to apologise to Brigadier Willie Pike for not getting him to his meeting. He did appear, though, to be somewhat relieved to be back in one piece.

In December, leading up to Christmas, the Chinese made peaceful overtures to us, though in fact it was mainly propaganda. We and the forward observers would often after dawn see in no man's land Christmas trees, which were festooned with presents. These were approached with some trepidation by our patrols, due to the likelihood of them being booby-trapped. We did not reciprocate. The Chinese often dabbled in propaganda. They would sometimes leaflet our units with extremely naive ideas of democracy, and tried to convince some of our soldiers that their wives were misbehaving at home. This, needless to say, had not the slightest effect on the Commonwealth soldier. They would also sometimes fly a small biplane at night to fly over our positions with loudhailers shouting out propaganda. The pilot was known as "Bed Check Charlie". We often wondered what we would do if we met this aircraft, as we were armed only with a .38 pistol. Equally, we often flew leaflet drops to try to persuade the Chinese of the error of their ways. These sorties were not popular, as we had to fly the whole of the divisional front at a height of 1,000 feet above their forward trenches. It was like disturbing a hornets nest and seemed not to produce any tangible results. Once the Australian Regiment were holding a vital position near point 355, and the two sides were literally within hand-grenade throwing distance of each other. On one night the Chinese brought up a loudhailer and shouted at the Australians: "We are coming to get you Aussies." The diggers' response was typical: "Then bring your own grog."

King George VI died on 6 February 1952, and the division marked this sad occasion by firing a 101-gun salute by the British, New Zealand and Canadian Field Regiments. Orders were given that no other weapons were to be fired throughout this period, and the whole front fell totally silent. The BMRA, over the wireless, ordered a single gun from the 14th Field Regiment to fire one round onto a Chinese position. He then fired each of the other twenty-three guns in turn at 1-minute intervals, and then each regiment similarly in turn. This took an hour and 40 minutes. It was a very solemn occasion.

During this time we were getting very short of intelligence about the enemy facing us, and the division was mounting many night attacks up to company level on the enemy positions with the main aim of bringing back a live prisoner. One such attack had been made on the centre of the front. They got on to the enemy hill quite quickly but the Chinese infantry were dug in, four storeys deep, and dawn was breaking before the attackers had got down to the third floor and so they were forced to retire with no prisoner. They were then caught in the open and in no man's land in daylight trying to get back, and were being heavily mortared and shelled by the Chinese. I had taken off before dawn to try to quieten down the enemy shelling and help the company get back. The cloud base was about 500 feet and the company's base position was on a hill nearly 200 feet high, so I only had about 300 feet in which to fly above the company position. The Chinese were heavily engaging it with 122-mm medium guns. All I could do was to fly continuous steep turns above the position and engage any targets that I could see through the heavy rain and in front of the company trying to get back. Whilst I was doing this, a Chinese medium 122-mm shell burst directly underneath me and a splinter from the ground burst went through the door of the aircraft, luckily with not too much damage.

During these flights I usually carried the flight camera. This was an RAF F24 camera about 2 feet high, and I normally had it fixed instead of the rear seat so that I could take oblique photographs whenever I wished. I had a foresight and backsight fitted to the wing strut on the port side, so that if I saw an active gun position I could line the aircraft up on it. I then did a simple sum of air speed and height on my knee pad, and took one photograph, followed in so many seconds by another, thus giving me a stereo pair. On landing, my RAF corporal (Cpl) photographer would immediately take out the camera and retire to his darkroom, which was in a 3-ton truck, and develop the prints. By the time I had driven back to the flight headquarters he had handed me the wet prints, which I delivered immediately to the Divisional Counter Bombardment Officer. Having decided the exact position of the enemy gun, it was then added to the counter bombardment list for destruction at a later date. Using this method we managed to establish a comprehensive list of all the enemy gun positions facing us.

About once a fortnight I had the camera fitted in the vertical position, and I would fly the front from the left to the right two or three times, producing a complete vertical cover of stereo prints, which were then delivered to the intelligence staff, who found them of inestimable value, as they had no other source of aerial photography. The disadvantage of this to me was that I permanently had a 1-foot round hole in the side and in the bottom of the aircraft, which let in copious amounts of cold air.

It was at this time that we frequently had to fly south to either Seoul airport or Kimpo, just to the west, to collect pilots or passengers or badly needed spares. The only radio we carried was an Army 62 set, which was incapable of speaking to any air traffic controllers in the country, so we were entirely on our own. We would fly over the airport and inevitably we always got a red Aldis lamp from the control tower, denying us permission to land, so we had to resort to desperate measures. We would fly to the beginning of the runway to the left side and do steep turns at about 50 feet and watch the long line of heavy four-engined transport aircraft trying to land in a stream on Seoul city airport. We would wait until there was a slight gap between two aircraft and then do a very short landing on the end of the left of the runway so as to avoid the slipstream of the aircraft landing in front of us, and then turn off at the first intersection before the aircraft landing behind caught us up. It was an unnerving way to land, and got the American air traffickers extremely angry with us, but there was no other way. One day the flight commander landed, but was still going too fast as he turned off at the first intersection and managed to collapse the starboard undercarriage, to his great embarrassment. On another day, I had similarly landed at Seoul and was taxiing into dispersal when I was directed to park by a very large black American airman. He wanted me to park behind a big four-engined US transport aircraft with twin tail booms and which had the rear doors open. I stopped just short of this aircraft and carried out the usual drill of stopping the engine, which was to turn off the two ignition switches and at the same time put on full throttle, which would clear the cylinders. The engine was supposed to stop immediately, but this time it roared into life and the aircraft leapt forward. The American airman was not seen for dust and, before I could stop the aircraft, my propeller was going round inside the doors of this enormous transport aircraft. I realised that I had a faulty magneto and could not stop the engine. My only course of action was to turn off the fuel and wait for nearly four minutes until both the carburettors had run out of fuel.

Kimpo airfield housed three or four American Sabre jet squadrons and also an Australian Squadron of Meteors, and at one time a South African Squadron of Mustangs. We would adopt a similar procedure that we used at Seoul city airport, except that this time we inevitably arrived as whole jetstream was taking off on operations, to fight Russian-built MIGs over the Yalu, and we would end up doing steep turns for up to half an hour, waiting for the last aircraft to get into the air. By this time, if you were unlucky, the first stricken aircraft, which had been hit over the Yalu, were beginning to crash-land all over the strip, so we had to wait until they had finished before we could eventually manage to land. Again, after a fashion, it did work.

Perhaps I should explain how these magnetos worked. The Gypsy major engine had two magnetos, which provided the spark to ignite the fuel in the cylinders. When starting the engine, the drill was to tell the ground crew by a thumbs-up sign that the switches were on. He would then swing the propeller and start the engine. Once started, you had to put each switch off in turn. If there was a change in engine note it signified a faulty magneto and you could not fly. Though we did have a battery, it had a very small capacity, so we only used it if we were on our own. Not infrequently, having put a passenger into the back seat and got him strapped in, you then started up and then found that you had a faulty magneto. You then had to switch off the engine, undo your straps, get out, open the engine cowling to get at the offending magneto, then scrabble in the ditch to find a stone about the size of your fist. You then struck the magneto with a sharp blow to unstick it, replaced the cowling and got back into the cockpit, strapped in and restarted the engine. By this time, of course, the passenger, having watched this bizarre performance, had lost all interest in flying and only wanted to get out. You just ignored him and took off.

At about this time, the Chinese were holding large numbers of United Nations prisoners in prison camps in the north near the Yalu. Although there was no wire around the camps, they could not escape because of the harsh climatic conditions and the fact that there was no way they could pass themselves off as Asians. There was virtually no communication with these prisoners, so we had no idea as to their number and who in fact they were. The Foreign Office sent out a squadron leader to teach the six pilots and half a dozen forward gunner OP assistants each an individual secret code, which had to be memorised. These twelve were considered to be the men most likely to be captured in the division. The idea being that, if captured, they could perhaps write letters home via the Red Cross with details of other prisoners being held, in code. It certainly wasn't too good for our morale. In the event of course, none of us were captured. The only pilot to be captured had only recently arrived, and had not been taught a secret code!

As spring approached and the weather improved, we had visits by the occasional concert party. The most notable was Danny Kaye, who was a great anglophile. He stipulated that if he came out that he must be allowed to visit the Commonwealth Division. He arrived

Danny Kaye with Brigadier Pike, the Deputy Divisional Commander

56   Continuing operations: from December 1951

Concert party

with us and demanded to be flown over the front to see the Chinese. There was no way that we were going to be responsible for the demise of Danny Kaye, so the flight commander flew him in his Auster back and forth over our own gun lines at a fairly low height. He was mightily impressed by the large number of enemy guns, and was returned safely, none the wiser.

7
Counter-bombardment

From the beginning of 1952, it became clear that the United Nations, although having the capability of breaking the Chinese and advancing north towards the Chinese frontier, had clearly decided not to do so because of the extremely heavy casualties which would inevitably have been incurred. On the other hand, the Chinese were clearly still determined to break through the 8th Army and to fight south to Seoul and beyond. They always seemed happy to accept enormous casualties. To this end they continued for more than a year to launch frequent massive army and corps attacks by the seemingly inexhaustible use of infantry manpower preceded by extremely heavy artillery barrages. However, on the whole, the 8th Army, with the heavy use of artillery, was able to hold the present line. So, in effect, a stalemate was reached, and peace talks were started at Panmunjom, though it was over a year before they produced a ceasefire. No peace treaty has ever been signed, and technically today the United Nations are still at war with North Korea and its Chinese allies.

This strategy was, of course, replicated within the Commonwealth Division and we settled down to a fairly static warfare to contain the Chinese armies and to hold our positions. It therefore became to some extent an artillery war. We had two aims: the first was to neutralise and destroy the Chinese guns, and the second was to help to break up the massive infantry assaults on our positions, in order to prevent any breakthrough. This, of course, also affected the use of the Air OP. So our first objective became to destroy the enemy artillery, and our second to carry out general reconnaissance and to help break up attacks on our own infantry.

The divisional counter-bombardment officer wrote regular reports on the progress of the counter-bombardment battle. Attached as Annex I are extracts from one of these reports, which were distributed throughout the division, and it gives a good overall view of the use of the Air OP Flight and the vital part it played in the battle.

Sadly, in May 1952, we lost our first pilot, Captain Joe Luscombe of the Australian Artillery. He was doing a routine sortie over the front when his aircraft was

Joe Luscombe in the crew room waiting for a sortie

engaged and hit by small-arms fire. He lost radio contact and was next seen flying crab-wise over the strip, obviously in great difficulty. He managed to complete a very rough circuit of the strip, but as he finally turned on to the approach the aircraft stalled, fell into a steep dive and went into the wooded cliffs on the far side of the Imjin River. He was killed instantly. One bullet had gone through the 62 set radio, and one through the canvas, just ahead of the stern post, and had severed one of the two 1/4-inch thick rudder cables, so he had no lateral control of the aircraft whatsoever.

Although we had now started to fly higher and higher, we did not have parachutes until we were issued with an American back type parachute, and about six months later another aircraft flown by Captain Liston, of the Canadian Artillery, was hit by 37-mm LAA fire and a wing was severed. Both he and his observer parachuted safely and were captured by the Chinese. He had only just joined us and it was I think his first or second operational sortie.

The Chinese had about twenty to thirty 37-mm LAA guns on our front, whose main task was clearly to shoot down one of our aircraft. They were quite difficult to spot and they changed positions frequently, but we had a very good idea of most of their positions. We had evolved a tactic which kept their interference down to a minimum. If you heard the rounds or saw the red tracers then you immediately took evading action. You then called on the HQ RA command net: "6 Dog [my call sign] LAA fire map reference 4520 over." The BMRA would say: "Roger out to you, 43, Mike Target Mike Target Mike Target map reference 4520 scale three VT fire." Then, within 40 to 60 seconds, seventy-two 25-pounder shells from the Royal New Zealand Artillery Regiment would burst about 30 feet above the area of the open gun pit. This would neutralise them and they probably would not fire again that day. They only ever fired one burst at us at a time because they knew that if they continued to fire we would find their exact position, and they then faced not only immediate retribution, but probable destruction.

Just north of Kuhwa-ri, towards their supply areas, they also had some heavy anti-aircraft (HAA) batteries. I was once engaged by them and their first salvo burst immediately below me and the second above me. A very good bracket, so I quickly decided to find a less dangerous bit of sky.

For most of this year, the flight were being tasked with four destructive shoots on enemy guns, each day, each sortie, on average, taking 2½ hours. In effect, this meant that each individual pilot was flying one counter-bombardment sortie a day. This would be in addition to any other sorties he might be given. Most pilots were now flying between 50 and 60 hours a month.

The drill was to take off and net on to the "Persuader" Battery's radio, and they would then allocate one gun for the destructive task. The 8-inch gun fired a 200-lb

This photo, taken from 6,000 feet, shows a single field gun in the centre of the photo and two medium four-gun positions in the top left-hand corner, and it shows how difficult they were to spot

shell and was incredibly accurate. It could be corrected to 10 yards for range and 5 yards right or left. It would take about five or six ranging rounds to get the exact position. You then fired round after round until you eventually got a direct hit on the overhead cover above the gun. Even this was not guaranteed to destroy it, because they frequently built a thick concrete roof over the gun. You then would use the "concrete busting fuse", which would go through the concrete and hit the gun itself, causing its destruction. A sortie took up to 2½ hours and sometimes it took two sorties to destroy one gun. It could take eight days to completely destroy a four-gun medium or heavy battery. Sometimes, if you had not completed a shoot,

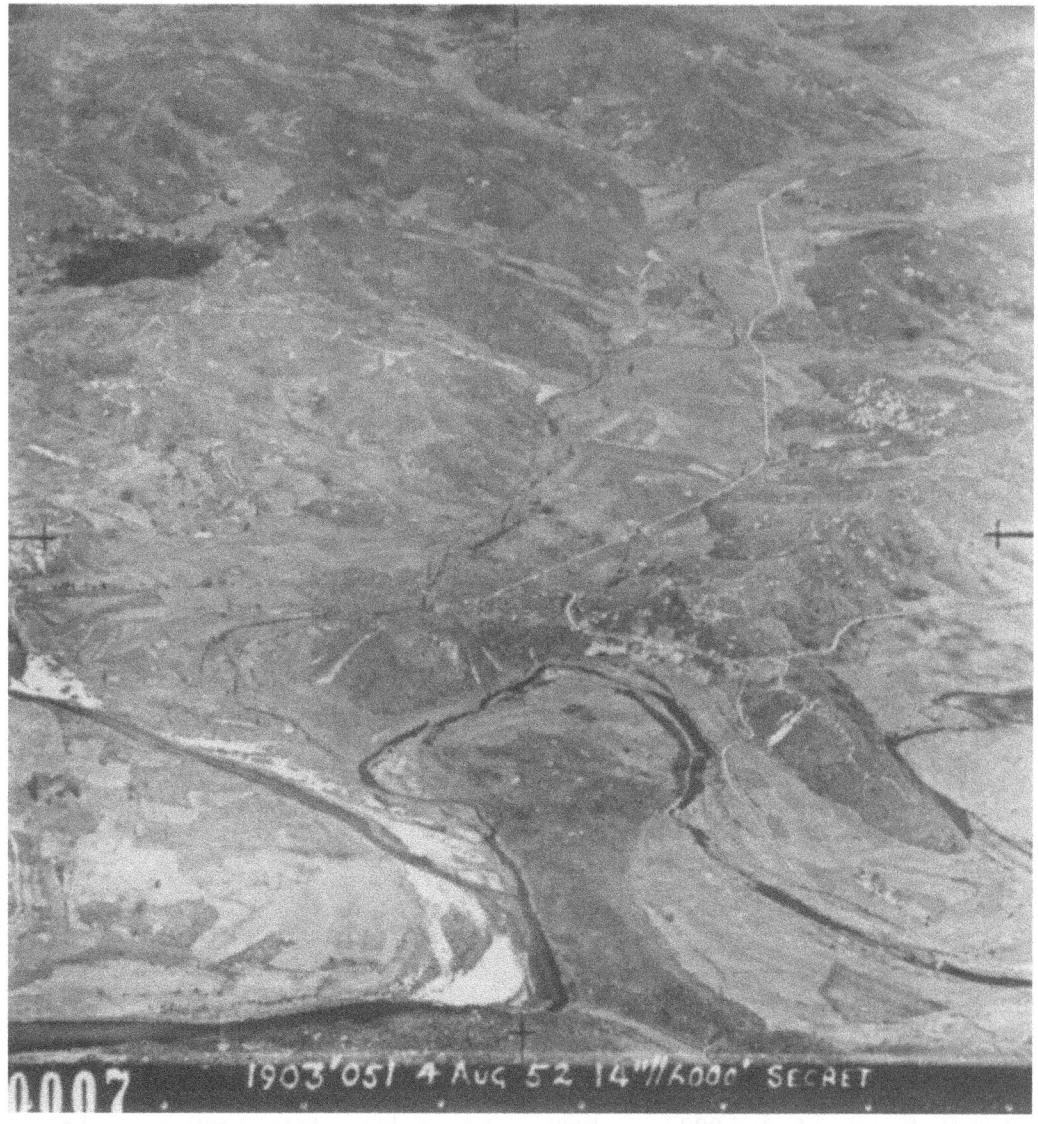

There are two gun positions in this photo

you would hand it over to the next pilot who would have been following your corrections over the air, whilst in the flight headquarters. On one occasion I was still conducting four separate shoots when I had to return to base. The next pilot took over from me in the air and completed all four shoots.

By this time we had discarded the very heavy issue binoculars and had bought from Japan some lightweight binoculars with much greater magnification. They were an enormous improvement and greatly increased our capability. On a routine reconnaissance of the divisional front, you would start at one end, put on half flap to reduce speed, and then line the aircraft up on the required heading. You then

There is one gun position in the centre of this photo

used both hands to hold the binoculars to scan the ground and flew the aircraft straight and level with your knees, 15 miles to the other end of the front. You then did exactly the same thing in the other direction.

At one stage we had discovered some enemy heavy batteries, which were way beyond the range of our guns and we could not rely on airstrikes to destroy them. So the CRA told the "Persuaders" to move a single gun forward to a map reference just behind one of the forward infantry battalions, into a sniping position, so that we could destroy these enemy guns.

Two photos of Chinese positions on point 169 in January 1952

The battery commander set forth in his jeep, followed by a large gun-towing vehicle and an 8-inch gun. Unfortunately, his map-reading skills were not what they might have been and he misread his map by a complete grid square to the north. A sentry in a forward position of the King's Shropshire Light Infantry, suddenly, early one morning, saw a US jeep passing his position and driving along a track leading north into the Chinese lines. Unfortunately, he was so surprised he did nothing about it. The battery commander probably had rice for dinner that night and was never seen again. Not long afterwards, the same soldier saw a large 8-inch gun approach his position, also heading north. This, fortunately, was too much for the light infantryman and he stopped it and sent it back south, thus saving one of our best assets.

During this time we were also given the support of a battery of 155-mm "Long Toms". These guns had an enormous range, but with a very high muzzle velocity, which gave them

Counter-bombardment 63

This photo shows the same position about two and a half months half later. This third photo, from 2,000 feet, clearly shows the extensive trenches of an enemy platoon and company position on point 169 on the centre of the front. These hills were originally wooded, but were now completely bare, due to the constant bombardment of our shells and mortars

a flat trajectory, and made them somewhat inaccurate. We used them to smarten up the enemy rear areas, headquarters and supply dumps. They certainly made life extremely difficult for the enemy rear echelons, and were a useful addition to our armoury.

Each of our battalions had an anti-tank platoon of four 17-pounder guns, which, as there was little enemy armour, did not have much to do. These guns similarly had a very high muzzle velocity, a low trajectory and a long range, like the US 155-mms.

64   Counter-bombardment

So we borrowed four of them and put them under the command of a gunner subaltern and fired them as a troop on a similar task to the "Long Toms".

During the year, 61st Light Regiment Royal Artillery, equipped with the 4.2-inch mortar, joined us. They had thirty-two of the 4.2-inch mortars, which greatly increased our available firepower. Due to their relatively short range, we did not use them that often; they were mainly used by the forward OPs in direct support of the infantry, although occasionally we did bring them in on our divisional targets if they were within range.

One day I was flying an evening sortie when the Chinese launched an army attack with two divisions on point 227, on the western slopes of point 355. These hills, which were of great strategic importance, were always hotly contested and often changed hands. The Chinese opened up at dusk with the usual heavy artillery barrage, and I was engaging live enemy batteries when I suddenly saw gun flashes only about 300 to 400 yards directly in front of our forward positions, which were then being attacked. The gun flashes were from four 122-mm self-propelled guns dug into deep pits, but with no cover apart from camouflage nets. They must have dug these pits and installed the tracked guns and camouflaged them the night before. They had done this so skilfully that the ground OPs with the forward infantry completely failed to spot them throughout the next day. I immediately put a regiment of 25-pounders firing airburst on to them, and I continued for some time until they had completely stopped firing. The next morning the gun pits were empty and the tracks of the guns could be seen going away to the north. They were very brave gunners indeed, but they certainly paid a heavy price and, as far as I am aware, they never tried this trick again.

8
Operations to the end of 1952

We frequently used to fly down to Projectile strip in order to liaise with the Corps Air OPs who sometimes operated in support of us. After such a visit, we would sometimes fly a low pass over the strip in farewell. One day, one of their pilots decided to reciprocate on the Fort George strip. Unfortunately, he failed to see the 18-foot-high solid copper aerial above our command post and hit it with his port wing. He landed again somewhat sheepishly. The metal of the forward edge of his port wing was like corrugated paper. However, we decided it was still airworthy so he flew back to his base. His explanation on arrival for this damage was that he had been hit by enemy LAA fire over the front. To our utter amazement his masters believed this story and he was from then on feted as a very brave pilot!

Bob Warner with me in the back seat visiting the US Air OPs on Projectile strip

By the end of 1951, only three of the original pilots remained – Ronnie Gower, Arthur Stewart Cox and myself – and we had a number of new pilots over the following year, namely John Crawshaw, Bob Warner, Jerry Joyce, Brian Forward RAA and Bob Liston CDN, who lasted less than a week. He was replaced by Mike Tees CDN. My replacement was "Warby" Warburton, who remained for only three weeks and then went back to Malaya.

Throughout our time in Korea, two of our biggest problems were the maintenance of the aircraft and the difficulty of obtaining spares. We could only do daily maintenance at the forward strips, and any aircraft needing second- or third-line maintenance meant that our only alternative was to fly the aeroplane back to Japan, almost regardless of the state it was in. Unfortunately, priority was given to the Malayan Emergency, that being a British interest as opposed to the United Nations interest in Korea. So 656 Air OP Squadron in Malaya was given priority over spares. This did sometimes get quite critical. We were always damaging the wooden propellers, and at one stage the next aircraft to damage a propeller was

66 Operations to the end of 1952

going to be operationally grounded. Only a flash signal from the general to HQ Far East Air Force finally solved the problem, and six propellers were flown up from Singapore in the Air Officer Commanding's (AOC) Hastings.

At one stage I had to fly for nearly three months without the three basic flying instruments: an airspeed indicator, a turn and bank indicator, and a rev counter. I was only able to do this because we did have 600 yards to land on and by that time I was a fairly experienced pilot, so it really was a case of "flying by the seat of one's pants". Of course, in peacetime one would not have been allowed into the air if just one of these instruments was not working. There was a small stores section under a flight lieutenant in Iwakuni, but this had a very small number of spares, most of which were for the Sunderland flying boats. The only real source of spares was in Singapore.

Though sometimes we felt that we had difficulties over spares, compared to some of our allies we were extremely well equipped. An illustration of this was that one day the divisional commander, Major-General Jim Cassels visited the 1st Republic of Korea Division who were on our flank. He was ushered into the Divisional Command Post, which was dug in, very deeply, in a hill. He went into an extremely dark cave lit by one candle and all he could see was the Korean divisional commander sitting at a six-foot table, where he joined him. He was fascinated to see that the only item on the table was one field telephone which had no wires attached to it. As his eyes became used to the gloom, he saw that there were dozens of Korean soldiers sitting on their hunkers and facing the wall of the cave. Suddenly one of them leapt to his feet, came over to the table and fixed two wires to the telephone, which he then handed to the Korean general. Major-General Cassels then realised that each of these men was holding a live telephone cable in each hand, so that if anyone rang they got a small electric shock, and they then connected the wires to the general's telephone. Having few field telephones, they just used soldiers, which were in much more plentiful supply. Our petty shortages of equipment paled into insignificance.

Farewell drinks party for Major-General Cassels, at Divisional Headquarters

1903 Flight early 1952: pilots from left, Bob Warner, Arthur Stewart-Cox, Ronnie Gower, Derek Jarvis, and John Crawshaw. Joe Luscombe had just been killed

This army was extremely short of even basic equipment, but still managed to fight the Chinese fairly successfully.

At about the end of July 1952, Major-General Cassels handed over command of the division to Major-General Mike Alston-Roberts-West. The division gave him a farewell cocktail party, which was held at divisional headquarters.

I have previously mentioned my bright idea of using salt to get rid of the ice on my aircraft in the winter. By midsummer this finally came home to roost. I was doing a pre-flight check one day and banged my hand on the underside of the wing. To my horror it knocked a hole in the fabric. I called the flight sergeant, who looked at the hole and punched it hard with his fist, which went straight through the wing and came out on the top. Quite clearly, the whole fabric of the aircraft was completely rotten. It was just like a wet rotten potato sack, and quite clearly was in no fit state to fly. But, as I've explained before, we neither had the kit nor the expertise to completely re-fabric an aeroplane on the strip. So next morning I set off with my airframe mechanic to fly this wreck the 500 miles back to Iwakuni in Japan. Luckily the weather was not too bad, but of course I had to fly around every cumulus cloud I saw because I dare not risk flying into heavy rain, which would no doubt have completely taken the fabric off and the aircraft would have simply dropped out of the sky. We did, however, manage to reach Japan and I spent a day with my crew stripping off the rotten fabric. The next day, however, I had to leave it to them and fly a brand new aircraft, which had just been delivered, back north to Fort George.

On the Auster, there are a number of places where there are two 8-inch zip fasteners, which when pulled back allowed you to grease and carry out maintenance inside the aircraft. Leading Aircraftsman (LAC) Howe called me over one day when he had opened a pair of these zips at the rear of the aircraft and asked me to have a look. Just in front of the stern post I saw a swallows' nest with two eggs in it, sitting happily on the two rudder control cables. We carefully checked the rudder's performance but there seemed to be no problem, so we left the nest there until the eggs hatched and the chicks flew off. This aircraft was airborne for up to 5 to 6 hours a day, yet it seemed to be of no concern whatsoever to the birds who successfully raised their brood.

In the summer we were visited by the new Commander in Chief (C in C) General Mark Clark, who arrived with a large retinue in a fleet of L19s, or "Bird Dogs". He was greeted by the divisional commander and by the pipes and drums of the King's Own Scottish Borderers and a guard of honour provided by the King's Shropshire Light Infantry. He was briefed by Major-General Cassels before visiting the division. Both these units were regularly involved in heavy fighting, but nevertheless managed to put on an extremely smart parade for the general.

The United States Air Force (USAF) deployed a number of light helicopters known as "Whirly Birds"; these were used mainly on liaison flying, and in casualty evacuation. However, there was one dedicated unit, which was used solely to attempt to rescue downed pilots. If a UN aircraft had been shot down, then, provided there was a sighting of a live pilot on the ground, one of these choppers would be sent in to attempt a rescue. The downed pilot would usually be covered by UN fighter jets to keep the Chinese at bay during the rescue. This was an extremely dangerous operation, and many of the helicopters were themselves in turn shot down. However, provided

"Whirly Bird" Bell helicopter

that the original pilot was still alive they would continue to send in these helicopters to attempt a rescue. They were extremely brave pilots and their repeated attempts at rescue were a great morale boost to all UN pilots. We always knew that, in similar circumstances, we could rely on these US choppers to try to rescue us.

SAC Smith, engine mechanic. He kept my aircraft airworthy for over a year

The flight was probably flying much more during the summer and autumn, as there was more daylight and the weather was on the whole good. In June, for example, the flight flew about 320 hours and conducted around 300 shoots, most of which were trying to destroy the enemy artillery.

During the summer we had a visit from Field Marshal Lord Alexander and the Minister of State for War, Selwyn Lloyd. They arrived with the usual entourage in a fleet of light aircraft and were briefed by the Commonwealth divisional commander outside the flight headquarters. Before leaving for a tour of the division, they left their briefcases behind and I was placed as an officer guard on them until they returned.

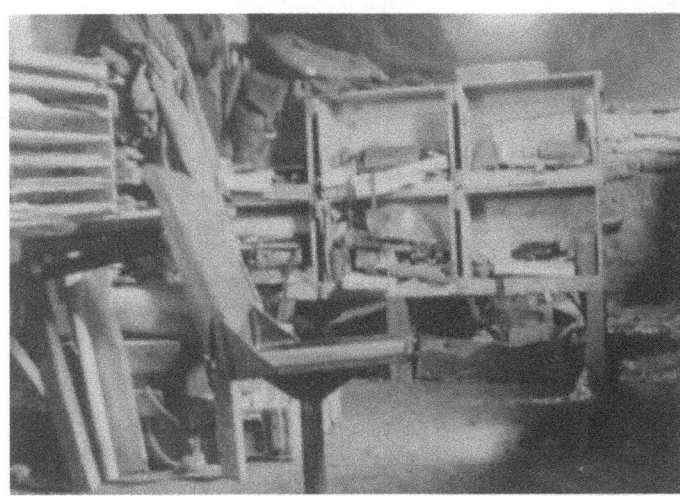

Pilots' crew room

The flight fired many thousands of rounds from the 16th Royal New Zealand Artillery Regiment. They always boasted that they were "amateur gunners". In point of fact they were an extremely efficient regiment. They had one endearing quirk, however, in that whenever you finished firing at a target with them and reported that the target was

These oblique photos, which I took from 2,000 feet, show the Chinese forward positions in the centre of the divisional front. The Chinese anti-tank ditches can be seen at the bottom left of the pictures and the Chinese trenches are on top of all the bare hills. We supplied the divisional intelligence staff with photos such as these of the whole divisional front on a weekly basis

neutralised or destroyed, they would acknowledge and then immediately report: "Shot, one for B echelon out." They had just added 1,000 yards extra range and fired another round of gunfire without any orders whatsoever from the pilot, hoping to catch the Chinese in their rear areas. One just had to remember this and keep out of that bit of sky. On 26 November 1952, at a small ceremony, the divisional commander fired their 300,000th round. The flight also fired thousands of rounds from the 25-pounder guns of the 2nd Royal Canadian Horse Artillery Regiment.

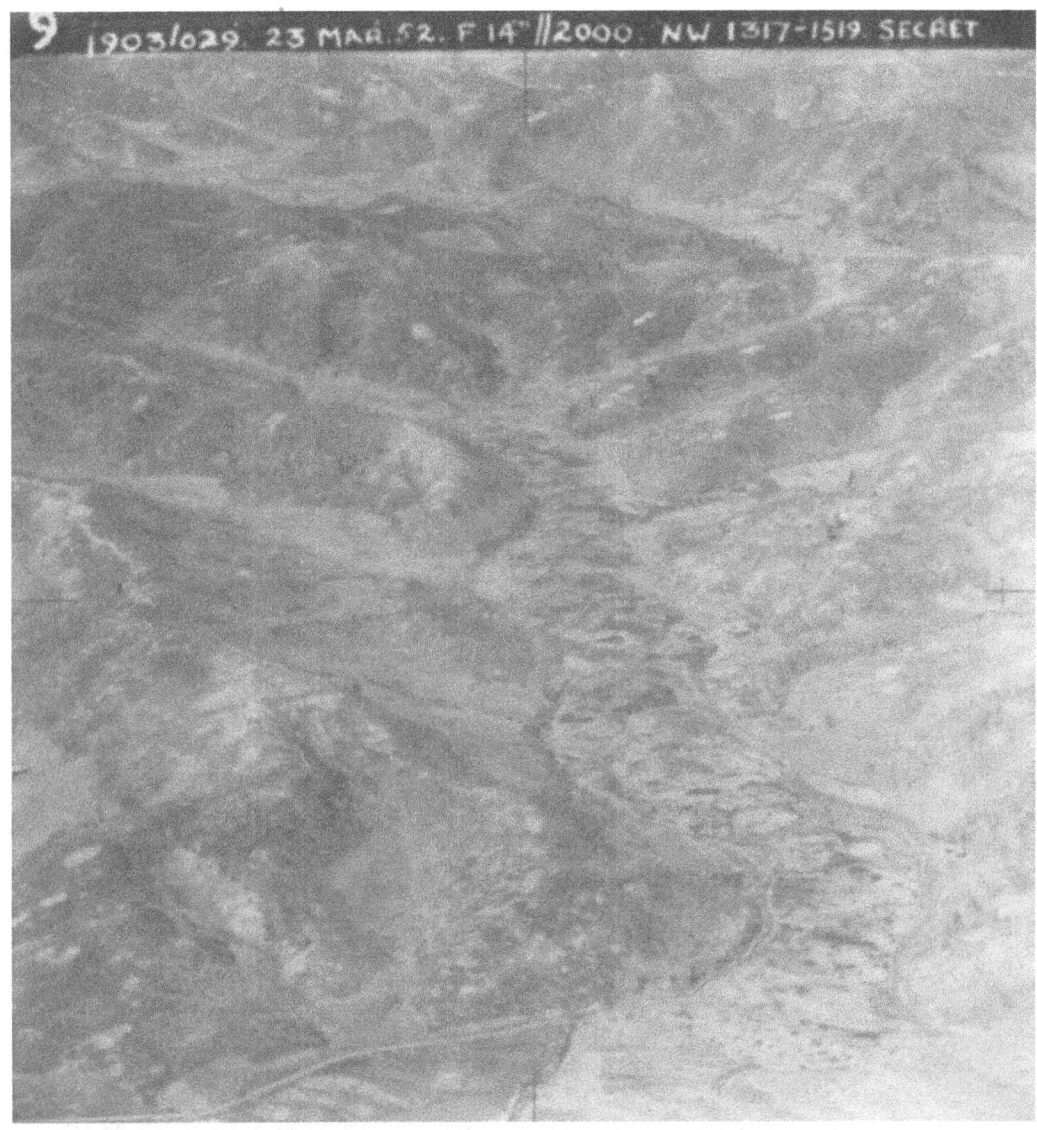

Major Ronnie Gower had finished his three-year Far East tour and left on 1 July 1952, after a year on operations, and handed over to Major Jack Hailes. In June 1952, the CRA told Captain Arthur Stewart-Cox and myself that whenever we decided that we had done enough flying he would give us both, as captains, command of a troop in the 14th Field Regiment. We were still only acting captains, and as regular officers this was a great opportunity. Arthur Stewart-Cox took command of a troop in June 1952. I soldiered on for a bit and then asked to be released in late July/August, only to be told that no replacement pilot could be found and that I had to continue flying. The CRA, on hearing this, ordered me to leave the country and go on leave for three weeks. As I always flew him I thought that he felt he had a vested interest! The only leave you got in Korea was five days R&R in

Kiwi gunners getting into action in winter 1951

2nd Royal Canadian Horse Artillery Regiment in action

a 12-month tour. I had already had my R&R and was then on my thirteenth month of operational flying.

So, on 8 August I was flown down to Seoul and picked up the daily courier, a Dakota, to Iwakuni in Japan. There I hitched a lift on a Royal Australian Air Force Dakota which had to fly back to Sydney to have a major overhaul. The aircraft had a large spare fuel tank fitted in the fuselage behind the pilot's bulkhead. This had a small leak, and petrol ran down the fuselage and out through the rear door, next to which was a small electric cooker, which we used to cook our lunch on. There was just the pilot and four or five passengers in canvas bucket seats.

We set off early one morning and flew south to Iwo Jima in the north Pacific. This was only a small atoll with an airstrip, and was where the US marines fought one of their most famous battles during the Second World War. Having spent the evening in the officers' club, the skipper then produced a steel keg of Australian beer, which we had to finish between us. It seemed that any aircraft flying up from Sydney would carry eight such kegs of the "amber nectar". One was to drink at each

Iwo Jima airstrip

The RAAF Dakota and a Japanese 75-mm gun

stop, and one was to be left behind for the next aircraft flying south. An extremely practical arrangement.

We continued flying next morning, having had little sleep, south to Guam. This was quite a large US base, where I was amazed to see the American soldiers wearing solar topis, khaki shirts and shorts, and long puttees. The evening was spent in much the same way, except that we could not find a spigot to fit the keg. We disconnected a large number of water taps before we found one that fitted, much to the Americans' annoyance, as it somewhat reduced their reserves of water.

These were long flights over the featureless Pacific Ocean, and we had no flying aids, radar or air traffic control. The skipper had to rely solely on his basic skill at dead reckoning air navigation. Luckily he was an extremely experienced pilot, who had been a pre-war King's Cup air racer. He had left the RAAF after the Second World War, but re-enlisted for the Korean War.

The next leg was a long one to Momote, a tiny atoll in the South Pacific in the Admiralty Islands. It had a small airstrip which had been resurrected for the Korean War. The island was almost uninhabited; there was only one Australian major and six troopers. They had one Centurion tank, which was still on the secret list, and had been shipped out from United Kingdom. They spent their time driving this tank round and round the island doing tropical trials. The major looked after us extremely

The airstrip on Momote near Manus in the Admiralty Group; loading before taking off for Townsville

well and, of course, the inevitable keg was produced.

The next day we flew on to Townsville in northeast Australia. This was a very long leg and we had to cross Papua New Guinea. We reached the Owen Stanley mountain range, which was beyond the point of no return, and we had no option but to fly through the mountain pass. Unfortunately, there was 8/10 cloud, and we flew through at 8,000 feet, occasionally getting glimpses of 13,000 foot peaks on either side. A hair-raising experience, but our doughty pilot seemed utterly unconcerned. Luckily we got through, and eventually made it to Townsville.

Townsville was a small sub-tropical town with one dirt Main Street, wooden sidewalks and swinging bar doors; more like Texas. The night was again spent emptying a keg. We were about to take off the next morning when the port engine caught fire, luckily before we were airborne. The RAAF produced two engine mechanics who looked at it and said that it was the wrong mark of engine and that two more mechanics would have to be flown up from Sydney to fix it. However, that afternoon, a subaltern of the Australian Signals Regiment appeared from Woomera in the outback, where the UK was conducting rocket trials, and asked the skipper for a lift to Sydney. When he was told that the port engine had caught fire, he immediately said that he was an electrician and that he would try to mend it, so we gave him a set of dungarees and he spent the whole night working on the engine and next morning said that it he had fixed it! So we all piled in and started up, there was no fire, and we continued to fly the last thousand miles to Sydney.

I spent a day in Sydney and managed to visit the parents of Joe Luscombe and gave them my condolences over his sad death. The next day I was met by an Australian Air OP pilot from their one flight, in an old Auster Mark III. He flew me down to Canberra and they put me up in their mess and were extremely hospitable. I gave them a long talk on the operations of 1903 Flight in Korea. After seven days, I rang the RAAF, only to be told that the Australian battalion had taken heavy casualties, and that the aircraft which I'd hoped to return on to Japan was filled with reinforcements and they could not find me a seat. This meant that the only way I could get back to Japan was to buy an airline ticket with Qantas. On a captain's pay this was nigh impossible. However, they rang me back the next day and said that there were so many casualties that they were having to put on a second aircraft and that they could get me back, but I had to leave in two days. Needless to say, I accepted and flew civil back to Sydney and then flew back across the Pacific Ocean in a Dakota, the same trip in reverse, including kegs, to Iwakuni.

When I got back to Iwakuni I still had about eight days' leave left, but found that the flight was still a pilot short as the Canadians had not yet replaced the pilot who had been shot down. I went into the mess and, much to my surprise, met Brigadier Pike. He asked me what I was doing, and I explained that I had just got back from Australia and that I had booked myself on the courier to Seoul the next morning, as the flight was still short of a pilot. He glared at me and said: "I told you to go on three weeks' leave. You will stay in Japan for the next week." The only time in my career I have received a stern telling off for arriving back from leave early. So I was able to spend an interesting week touring Japan.

Throughout the year there was continuous heavy fighting on the right of the front, and many desperate battles were fought over point 355 and its western slopes of Matthew, Luke and John.

In August 1952, having just brought a new aircraft back from Japan, I was doing a normal reconnaissance of the front at 2,500 feet when the engine suddenly lost power and I could only get idling revs. I glided back towards our own lines and I just managed to cross the line on the western part of the front. There was a small lateral dirt road which I could just about reach. As I approached to land, a Canadian 2½-ton truck was going along it in the same direction as myself. Luckily, he was going faster than me and then disappeared around the next bend. I managed to make a good forced landing, and then a jeep came round the bend towards me travelling extremely fast with four soldiers of the King's Own Scottish Borderers in it. The driver panicked, slammed on his brakes and stopped in the middle of the road. I was still doing about 30 mph and had the choice of hitting the jeep and possibly killing the soldiers or putting the totally undamaged aircraft into the ditch. I put on hard right rudder and brake and put the aircraft into a 6-foot ditch. The terrified jeep driver promptly drove off and left me there.

Point 227, Mathew, Luke and John; not a vestige of vegetation left

I got out of the wreck somewhat shaken but otherwise unhurt and was putting up a jury aerial so that I could radio the flight when another jeep arrived. It was driven by the padre of the Vingt-Deuxième Regiment du Canada. We had a totally useless conversation, as his command of English was even worse than my schoolboy French. He then left me and drove off. He did not turn out to be the good Samaritan, which I had hoped for! However, soon after yet another jeep appeared with two military policemen from the Provost Company. They said that they had seen me fly down into the next valley, but that I did not seem to reappear as usual, so they came to look for me. They soon sorted me out and put me in the jeep, and took me back to the flight. We never did discover what was wrong with the new engine, but I never flew that aircraft again. The next day a Divisional Order was published to say that if any driver in the division was confronted with an aircraft on the road in front of them, he was immediately to drive his vehicle off the road.

It was normal practice that, if you had an accident, then in order to keep your nerve you were expected to get back into the air again as soon as possible. So I took off again that afternoon and conducted a single gun destructive shoot with the "Persuaders", which took me 2 hours and 40 minutes.

Finally, about 20 September, a replacement pilot for me arrived from 656 Squadron in Malaya. He was a very well-known wartime pilot, who had re-enlisted for Malaya, but I had to teach him gunnery for four days as he was, to say the least, somewhat rusty. In fact, after three weeks, he was sent back to Malaya. I did my last 3-hour flight on 25 September, when I engaged two destructive shoots with the "Persuaders".

In summary, I had flown on operations for 14 months and had done $639\frac{1}{2}$ hours of operational flying, flown one night operation and carried out 60 night landings, 360 sorties and 302 airshoots. 1903 Flight, with never more than six pilots at any one time, was in action for two years, and in that time was awarded one Distinguished Service Order, thirteen Distinguished Flying Crosses, one US Air Medal and two Mentions In Dispatches. A quite remarkable record.

This ended my tour of flying as a gunner Air Observation Post Pilot. The next day I was still a gunner Observation Post officer, but this time with my feet firmly on the ground.

9

Three months as an Observation Post officer on the ground

The day after my last flight, I collected my OP party from the 13th Martinique Battery of the 14th Field Regiment, and went south to rear divisional headquarters. The 1st King's Liverpool Regiment had just arrived from Hong Kong and were doing their final training at the Divisional Battle School. I joined one of their companies on their last three-day exercise as a forward Observation Post officer, on my feet and carrying my communications. After the exercise I went back north and reported to the adjutant of the 14th Field Regiment, a friend of mine. He welcomed me to the regiment and said that I was to command Fox Troop and that I was to go up the line that night to take over 75 OP from the 16th Royal New Zealand Regiment. He then said: "Oh, by the way, don't unpack your kit." I said: "Basil, I do know about the 14 bus and have already left my kit with the Battery B echelon." The CO Lieutenant-Colonel Jack Slade Powell had an inflexible rule, which was that if any officer in the regiment of any rank made a mistake for whatever reason, he would immediately be sacked. This meant that he got on to the 14 bus and left the division for Japan immediately: no arguments. The 14 bus was known throughout the division, and consequently our infantry had the greatest confidence in the regiment and knew that we would never let them down.

I found that the OP which I took over was little more than a poorly dug open hole on the forward slope in a company position overlooking the two forward platoons. It was both inefficient and dangerous.

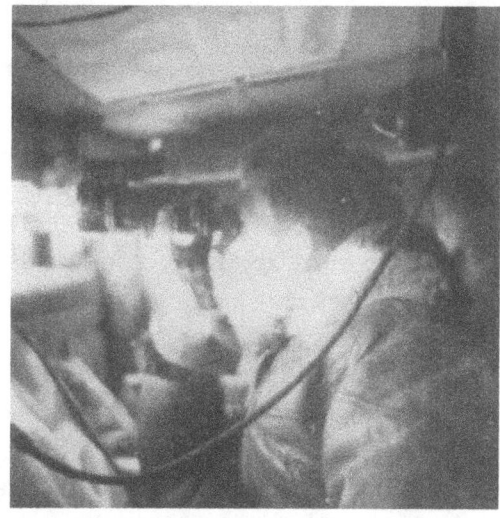

Original 75 Observation Post (above); the new Observation Post (right)

Aerial views of the enemy positions in front of me

During that night I and my OP party covered the whole position with a camouflage net, so that we could work under it in daylight. Having dug a second OP next to it, we put the spoil into the old hole. We then put in a parapet of two huge logs with an aperture about 3 feet long and 1 foot high and then roofed the hole over with two cross layers of logs, two feet of earth and a stone covering to make any shells burst on top rather than penetrating the roof. This took us four days. Each night, we had to march back to the reserve company areas, a round trip of about 3 miles, to carry up on wooden A frames on our backs, heavy radio batteries, radios, a charging engine, petrol, rations, a telephone exchange and various other pieces of equipment. An exhausting four days but well worth it, as we ended up with

a really well built and relatively safe and comfortable OP. We then had to dig an OP base on the reverse slope of the company position to house the men, rations, radios, charging engine and telephone exchange and various other bits and pieces. It all took some time.

We then dug a 15-foot deep communication trench from the OP running back through the hill to the OP base on the reverse slope. We collected all the various telephone lines which were lying in the open and re-laid them in the bottom of this trench so that they were relatively immune to shellfire. Similarly, we had to put remote cables from the OP base to the telephones and headsets in the OP and also in the Company Headquarters, which was dug deep into the centre of the hill, and was where I would sleep at night. A 25-pounder cartridge case heater was put

82 Three months as an Observation Post officer on the ground

Panoramic view from 75 Observation Post

into the OP and a chimney made of cartridge cases was laid back through the deep trench. It had holes all along it, so that any smoke was dispersed and could not be seen by the enemy.

Normally in an OP one would draw a panoramic view of the whole front, showing the enemy positions with ranges to the various targets. I was not a very good draughtsman, so I got the RAF corporal photographer from the flight to come up one night and the next day take a series of photographs of the views from the OP, and also to make up a photographic panoramic view of the enemy positions facing us.

The week after we arrived, B Company of the 1st King's took over the position. I met the company commander in the command post and he asked me, much to my surprise, who I was and what was I doing there. I said that I was his gunner OP officer and that I was there to provide him with artillery support. He then said that he did not want my bed in his command post. I replied that I had to be next to him day and night in order to support the company. He had transferred to the British Army from the Indian Army on the partition of India. It was not an auspicious start!

For the next four days, I was in the OP all day long, and with my three gunners marched every night back through no man's land to bring up supplies, batteries, rations and fuel. We were exhausted. On the fifth night I was in my bed in the command post when we were attacked by the Chinese. I never left my bed, and

spent the whole night bringing down defensive fire tasks all around the company position. No Chinaman crossed our wire and they suffered considerable casualties. We had no casualties. From that night on our presence was greatly appreciated by the company and we never had to bring up our supplies again. It was all done by the company and their "gook" train of South Korean porters. We had at last established a proper relationship.

I had now established a routine. I spent all day in the OP watching the Chinese and, at night, from my bed in the command post, I provided prearranged fire support for the company's standing patrols in no man's land and fire support when requested by our fighting patrols, and also defensive fire targets around the company when required.

One day I had just occupied the OP, about an hour before dawn, and was enjoying a hot soup. We got a can of soup a day which, when you pulled a strip off the top of the can it set off an internal heater which produced a cup of steaming soup without any smoke. Suddenly, my commanding officer appeared, having walked up alone from the rear companies during the night. As it began to get lighter he first assured himself that I was not wearing a tin hat, most unofficer-like, that I was wearing a Herbert Johnson hat and that the chin strap was highly polished. He was a pre-war officer who set extremely high standards. He then asked me to show him on my map where all the defensive fire targets and the defensive fire SOS targets were. These were all pre-registered targets close to the company position, and the SOS targets were usually on our own wire and were only fired as a last resort when the enemy were actually on our own wire and were about to overrun us. He then told me to fire on one of the SOS targets. This was a battery task, and was behind the company and was almost on our own wire. I pointed this out and said that the infantry should be still in their beds as it was not yet "stand to". He said fire. I gave the necessary orders, and though we could not see the fall of shot it sounded as though both E and F troops had fallen in the right parish. However, he was not satisfied and told me to bring it in closer and fire again. So I ordered the guns to add 100 yards, which I was fairly certain would put the rounds almost on our own wire. We heard the first troop, which sounded okay, then there was a delay and the second troop sounded much quieter and had obviously fallen short, and was in no man's land, well behind us. We looked at each other and I said I thought that the extra 100 yards had probably altered the charge on the guns from charge 1 to charge 1 plus 1, and if so the gun position officer should have got a further correction for range from his range tables. I thought that he had probably not done this, hence the shortfall. He agreed with me and told me to get the battery commander (BC) on the telephone, which I did. He told the BC that the gun position officer (GPO) of E Troop had made a mistake and that he was to be sacked immediately. Unfortunately, he was probably the most experienced GPO in the regiment, but nevertheless he was on the 14 bus at once and was out of the division by noon and in Japan that night. However, a couple of months later, and under a new commanding officer, it was reluctantly agreed to get this officer back.

During the winter months, we had a great problem. We only got "meteor" reports on the weather about once a day and never in the late afternoon. At about dusk there was a sudden large drop in temperature of about 15–20°, which was impossible to accurately predict. The only solution was to adopt the "COs 600". So, at dusk every night we automatically added an extra 600 yards to every target. A rough and ready solution, but it did work fairly well and certainly stopped us shelling our own infantry by mistake.

When Lieutenant-Colonel Jack Slade Powell left, the regiment threw a farewell drinks party for him. During this party, which was held about midday, the regiment was presented with a solid silver model of a 25-pounder gun. The CRA had decreed about a year before that each gunner officer would donate £5 a month into a silver fund. It was a lot of money in those days but we had nothing else to spend our pay on. From then on any gunner unit leaving the division would get a piece of silver. 1903 Flight, after a year in action, were given a solid silver model of an Auster at this party. All the officers except a newly joined second lieutenant managed to get to the party. The warrant officers stood in for the officers and ran the regiment. During the party the guns were constantly firing, and indeed fired five regimental targets.

I was in the OP one day when the battery commander, Major Tug Wilson rang. He said "Dog Fox Charlie". I asked him to repeat it, and meanwhile was desperately looking for one of my defensive fire targets which might have had this name. He then said "D F C". He was trying to tell me that I had been awarded the Distinguished Flying Cross (DFC). Soon after I attended a divisional awards ceremony and was given the ribbon by the divisional commander.

In late October I had located an enemy OP in front of me which was causing some trouble, but I wasn't able to destroy it. One day he spotted me and started to range a single gun on to my OP. I was calling the fall of shot to my OP assistant when I realised that he had got a good bracket on me, so Gunner Parfitt and I had ignominiously to lie down in the bottom of the trench. The next round did in fact hit the OP just below the aperture, but luckily did not explode. I had to get a friendly sapper up that night to take it away and blow it up.

Major-General Jim Cassels presenting me with the DFC ribbon on Fort George airstrip

The armour had little to do in this type of static warfare, so they dug a number of their Centurion tanks into the hills near to the reserve companies on the top of the ridge line. I used one of these to engage this troublesome OP. Unfortunately, like all high-velocity guns it had a very flat trajectory, and its rounds used to pass only a few feet above the infantrymen's heads, much to their surprise. However, it did manage to quieten this annoying OP down.

After about three weeks, I called my GPO up to take over the OP for two days and I was able to go back and get to know my troop of about fifty men. I also, of course, had to take over the GPO's job and had to smarten up my technical gunnery skills in the command post.

The officers were not allowed to get out of touch with the problems that the gunners faced, so one day every month one gun was taken out of its gun pit and all junior officers in the battery did a couple of hours gun drill under a troop sergeant major. The gunners much appreciated seeing their officers being made to work so hard.

In early December, B Company was to be relieved by A Company. I, of course, remained in the OP. A night relief in the line is probably one of the most difficult

A Centurion tank of the 8th Queen's Royal Irish Hussars, dug in near a company reserve position

Fox Troop, numbers two and four guns; the detachment operated in two halves, one commanded by the sergeant and the other by the bombardier, so that one half of the detachment was firing the gun whilst the other slept; their sleeping quarters can be seen in front of number two gun

operations of war to carry out. The relief started about an hour after dark when A Company started to trickle forward from the rear. The B Company commander then took an extraordinary decision to take the incoming company commander forward into no man's land to visit the standing patrols. We did not hear of them for the rest of the night. He left a very young and inexperienced captain to conduct the complicated operation. It soon started to go pear-shaped. I was so concerned that I took command of the company relief operation for the rest of the night. Luckily the Chinaman did not intervene. If he had, we would have been in some considerable difficulty. The two company commanders returned just before dawn, after the operation was completed. I was more than happy to hand the company over to the new A Company commander, who, much to my relief, was a highly experienced company commander. We got on very well together from then on.

On 15 November 1952 I again took a rest from the OP and took over as GPO. About dusk on 16 November the Chinese put in an extremely heavy attack on the forward company of the Black Watch on the Hook position, which was on the left

Number one gun of Fox Troop 13 Martinique Battery out of action for maintenance. The quads, or gun towing vehicles, and ammunition vehicles and drivers were back at B echelon and were only called up if the Battery had to move; the Troop command post was behind the guns and well dug into the side of a hill; orders were passed to the guns by a Tannoy system

of the front. Immediately, the whole of the divisional artillery was engaged with help from the artillery of the 1st US Marine Division on our left and the US Corps Artillery. My troop were firing incessantly, and at one time the whole regiment was on the order "gunfire" for three hours, which meant that the guns are fired, re-laid and fired again as fast as is possible. Occasionally, the battery would be taken off defensive fire tasks and put on to counter-bombardment targets against the enemy guns.

The guns were all overheating, which meant that there was a severe danger of a premature explosion inside a hot barrel. So I had to take one gun out of action in turn and all the cooks and bottle washers in the battery were melting snow and pouring cold water over the hot barrels.

Although in about 35 degrees of frost, it was hot and exhausting work for the gun detachments. They continuously had to throw the empty cartridge cases out of the gun pits so that they had enough room to service the guns.

Every 3-ton vehicle in the regiment was mobilised and they were driving down to the ammunition depots at Tokchong north of Seoul and driving back fully laden onto the gun positions with full headlights on, then dumping their loads and off again south for more, throughout the night. The divisional artillery began to run out of high-explosive shells in the early hours of the morning and had to resort to air-burst shells. By dawn we had expended those, and only had smoke rounds left.

Fox Troop that night fired nearly 2,000 rounds from four guns, and the regiment a total of 11,890 rounds from the twenty-four guns, nearly 500 rounds per gun.

When dawn came the whole position was about 2-feet deep in 25-pounder brass cartridge cases. We then found that we had lost a gunner. It transpired that he had left his gun pit during the night for a pee and had been knocked unconscious by a flying cartridge case. Although the temperature was extremely low he survived. When we found him, he was covered by a heap of warm cartridge cases, which of course had kept him alive. He was back on his gun later that day.

The Black Watch spent most of the night fighting, and in their deep bunkers with the Chinese often on top of them. The gunner OP officer with A Company brought down the whole of the divisional artillery on to his own head, on and off, for most of the night. He was awarded an immediate Military Cross (MC) and the battery commander a Distinguished Service Order (DSO). A Company held their ground throughout the night and were finally relieved just before dawn by C Company of the Princess Patricia's Canadian Light Infantry. The total number of casualties on the Black Watch position was five officers wounded and one missing, thirteen other ranks killed, seventy-two wounded and twenty-four missing. More than a hundred enemy dead were found inside the company wire. They must have suffered many more casualties beyond the wire, but we never knew the total because they always took their dead away. This was the first Hook battle, and I believe there were two more later on, which were even more fierce and with an even greater expenditure of artillery.

By this time, the 14th Regiment had been in action for about a year and we were relieved by the 20th Field Regiment on Christmas Day 1952. We handed over our OPs on Christmas Eve and all officers went back to the gun positions. There was then a formal handover of all ten command posts to the new regiment at midday on Christmas Day. The CO ordered a final regimental target which went off in near record time and he then formally handed over command to the new CO. Similarly, I handed over my troop as soon as the guns stopped firing. The new regiment then took over and fired their first regimental shoot.

We then all got into the waiting transport, only to discover that the battery was one man short. The command post officer (CPO) rushed off to look for him. He was found drinking beer in the NAAFI "hoochi". He was lucky he did not have to fight on for another year. We then set off south to the railhead, where the regiment came together for the first time for over a year. We then entrained for the long journey

About to entrain at Tokchong: Aubrey Fielder, Gibbo, and Mike Hunter, the Medical Officer

On the train: Harry Pearson, Dougie Cook, Frank Ward, Peter Harrison

back to Pusan. There was no heating and not very many windows on the train, so we spent the whole time in our sleeping bags, still in our dirty uniforms, for what was our last freezing cold night.

We arrived in Pusan, and the day after Boxing Day we had our Christmas lunch, which traditionally was served by the officers. The soldiers opted for chicken and bully beef, as they were eternally fed up with turkey, which was the mainstay of the American C rations that most of them had been living on. The officers' mess was in a US Quonset hut, and after having fed the men we had a formal dinner night, still in our somewhat smelly uniforms. During the dinner, the CO called for the survey officer and told him to get his compass and to lay the silver 25-pounder gun, which was on the table, on point 355, where, of course, we had expended many thousands of rounds. We had no other silver, that having been left in Hong Kong over a year before. This became a regimental tradition, and was followed for many years afterwards at all regimental dinner nights.

Two days later, we embarked on a troopship for Hong Kong, where the regiment disembarked, but some of us carried on to the UK, having completed our three-year Far East tour.

Conclusion

So ended my flying tour as an Air OP pilot. I had a long leave in the UK, and then with all my experience in field artillery and having no knowledge whatsoever of heavy anti-aircraft guns, I was posted to the 60th Heavy Anti-Aircraft Regiment in Northern Ireland, first as a troop commander and later on as the adjutant.

Whilst on leave, I was told that I had been awarded an American Air Medal. First of all, I was privileged to receive the DFC from Her Majesty the Queen at Buckingham Palace, and some time later I received the US Air Medal at the US Embassy from an American general. This was in some contrast to the Palace, which was very formal. The Americans, after the awards ceremony, gave us an enormous buffet lunch and copious amounts of drink, so we were able to meet a lot of old friends who were also receiving American decorations, and had a tremendous reunion.

In 1954 I went to Middle Wallop to do a 10-day refresher flying course. Much to my surprise, my flying instructor was the same pilot who had relieved me in Korea. However, I did not go back to do a second flying tour but went instead to the Army Staff College in January 1955.

In 1965, I did do another 3-year tour with Army Aviation, but this time as a staff officer, flying a mahogany desk in the Ministry of Defence. I was responsible for all pilot posting onto training and to units throughout the Army, the recruitment of potential pilots, and all career planning and promotions. I was also heavily involved in the large expansion of Army Aviation and the introduction of unit flights to each regiment in the Royal Artillery, the Armoured Corps and the Corps of Infantry. Each regiment had their own light aircraft, usually flown by one of their own officers. I was also involved in the formation of the Army Air Corps, which, when the gunners stopped flying, took over all Army flying.

So, my recollections range from the gunners flying light and unarmed Air OP aircraft in the 1940s to the beginnings of the Army Air Corps of today. The Army Air Corp is now the fourth combat arm flying heavily armed Apache Attack Helicopters.

Conclusion 91

Miss Winifred Jarvis, my aunt, Captain Derek Jarvis, and Mr Michael Jarvis, my brother, at Buckingham Palace

The author receiving the US Air Medal at the United States Embassy in London

Annex I

Extract from a report by the Divisional Counter-Bombardment Officer, Major Thomas RA

The Chinese had some 100 enemy guns, ranging from 152-mm Soviet howitzers to 75-mm howitzers, which could bear on the divisional front, and daily incoming rounds sometimes rose to about 500, accompanied by ground action. Enemy gun and mortar positions were tunnelled into the hills. Shortage of medium and heavy corps artillery, and ammunition, restricted bombards and so put a premium on observed destructive shoots by the Air OP, which flew four CB sorties daily. Pilots were briefed and debriefed each evening personally by the divisional counter-bombardment officer (DCBO), who also briefed air strikes through the Air Liaison Officer at Headquarters Royal Artillery (HQ RA).

The main sources of information were the Air OP, air photos, sound-ranging and shelling reports (shelreps). The target of one shelrep per incoming round, other than during heavy enemy attacks, was regularly achieved. During the period of hostilities ending in July 1953, the DCBO published 573 daily CB intelligence reports (intreps), which were circulated widely throughout the division. They included details of enemy activity, areas shelled, type/numbers of guns, battery probably responsible, new locations obtained and source, and retaliation, including air strikes and targets engaged by the Air OP. Hostile batteries lists were published regularly and periodic anti-aircraft hostile battery lists were also issued showing positions down to anti-aircraft light machineguns (AA LMGs).

The CB organisation worked smoothly, but their unpretentious yet high standard of efficiency created problems for themselves, because enemy guns and mortars were kept constantly on the move. The CCF artillerymen must have done some prodigious digging.

Air OP

Prior to the arrival of 1903 Air OP flight (Major R. N. L. Gower RA) in July 1951, Captain R. Begbie, a trained pilot serving in the 11th Sphinx LAA Battery, had been

Extract from a report by the Divisional Counter-Bombardment Officer, Major Thomas RA

flying Air OP missions with the Americans, primarily for the 29th British Brigade, and had done good work. He was awarded an American Air Medal.

Although 1903 Air OP Flight was an RAF unit, all six pilots were gunner officers. The original six pilots who came with the flight in July 1951 were all British. They were seasoned pilots, with over 800 hours each in their logbooks, and this was soon reflected in the extremely high standard of operational efficiency which they displayed from the outset, and which had the admiration of the whole division. From early 1952 onwards, Australian and Canadian pilots also served in the flight.

Miraculously, even without tented hangers, a very high rate of aircraft serviceability was maintained during the freezing winter months, but pilots had to wear so much clothing in their unheated cockpits that they could hardly get in. In the hot, humid summers they sometimes flew in PT vests and shorts because of the enhanced heat of the sun through the canopies.

Total air superiority permitted the exploitation of the capabilities of the Air OP to the limits, and the first to do this were the pilots themselves. They took considerable risks – many in number, but none foolhardy. Unlike the American Air OPs, for the first year they had no parachutes. Sorties were 1½ to 3¼ hours in duration.

Up until early summer 1952 they flew in depth 5,000 yards behind enemy forward positions at heights of 3,000 to 5,000 feet. Thereafter, because of many hits from the greatly increased AA LMG and 37-mm LAA fire, which the CCF had moved forward, and the loss of two pilots, the fly line was adjusted to the line of the division's forward localities, but at heights of 6,000 to 8,000 feet. These heights were necessary to keep reverse slopes under observation, so giving early warning of attacks but, above all, for their CB tasks which the CRA had directed were to be the first priority.

They were the mainstay of the CB battle. Without them it would have failed. They operated on the HQ RA command net, so ensuring rapid dissemination of information, and flicked to the flight net only for time-consuming destructive shoots. Shoots with nominated regiments were conducted on the regimental net, but some shoots, if they were short and snappy and traffic permitted, were allowed on the HQ RA command net. Over the months they engaged innumerable hostile batteries with the 936th Field Artillery Battalion and the "Persuaders", whose 8-inch howitzers could accept corrections of 5 yards. When engaging deep enemy gun positions with the very long-range American 155 guns, "Long Toms", they sometimes had to fly on winter days at 13,500 feet. The cold was numbing.

During Operation Commando they performed the astonishing feat of maintaining continuous daylight cover across the divisional front for eight days, finding twenty definite gun locations and thirty-eight probables, and, during the first three days only, taking thirty shoots, including enemy guns and mortars.

The first pilot lost in May 1952 was Captain B. T. Luscombe (Australian) who had his rudder controls shot away deep over enemy territory, struggled back to the airstrip, but crashed trying to land. He was awarded a posthumous Mention In Dispatches. American back-type parachutes were issued in early August 1952. Within a week the second pilot, Captain J. M. Liston (Canadian), was shot down, parachuted and was taken prisoner.

Of the six original pilots, two were due to return to the United Kingdom after the defensive battles in November 1951 and were replaced. The remaining four, Major R. N. L. Gower, who had already received an immediate Mention In Dispatches for Operation Commando, Captain L. R. B. Addington, Captain D. B. W. Jarvis and Captain A. G. E. Stewart-Cox, were all awarded the DFC within a year. Captain Jarvis was also awarded the American Air Medal.

Major J. M. H. Hailes RA succeeded Major Gower as flight commander in July 1952, and maintained well the high standard of operational efficiency then prevailing. He did some courageous flying and was awarded the DSO. In all, during the two years of hostilities from July 1951 to July 1953, the flight won one DSO, thirteen DFCs, two American Air Medals and two Mentions in Dispatches. This achievement must rank highly, if not the highest, in the annals of the Air OP. The flight made a contribution to the success of the division's operations which was out of all proportion to their small numbers.

Air support

The United Nations Forces were supported superbly throughout the campaign by the 5th United States Air Force. In addition to American aircraft, air strikes on the divisional front were flown by a South African squadron and carrier-borne aircraft from the Royal Navy.

The air liaison officer, an experienced fighter pilot with his VHF sets to HQ 5th United States Air Force and aircraft over the front, was fully integrated with the HQ RA command post. He worked closely with the BMRA and the DCBO, and the machinery for mounting air strikes was very slick indeed. Target indication with smoke was provided by the divisional artillery when required. Air OPs often made observations on the accuracy of fighter passes on the target and these were picked up by the air liaison officer (ALO) from the HQ RA command net.

Annex II

Second report from the Divisional Counter-Bombardment Officer, Major Thomas RA

The most effective method of annoying enemy artillery is to engage them with observed fire, preferably using 8-inch shells. In some cases the enemy has been unwise enough to put his gun pits in full view from ground OPs, but generally speaking they are either extremely difficult targets to engage from the ground or out of sight altogether. This is where the Air OP comes in.

There are two Air OP units operating on our front. One is our own 1903 Air OP Flight RAF, and the other is the Corps, Air Section, formed by centralising the two L19 aircraft organic to each American Corps Artillery Battalion, and maintaining control under the Corps Artillery Fire Direction Centre. Our own Air OP flight is controlled by HQ RA, and at present its primary role is counter-bombardment.

The Air OP Flight consists of six Auster aircraft piloted by officers of the Royal Artillery, and maintained by ground crews of the RAF. Each aircraft carries a radio set for communication with HQ RA and with the artillery allotted for the engagement of targets. There is a seat for the observer, whose first duty is to watch for enemy aircraft. In this theatre this is a sinecure, so it is possible to carry a passenger on operational flights, though passengers who suffer from air-sickness are apt to be viewed with some disfavour by the long-suffering ground crew.

Although it would appear possible for the flight to maintain an aircraft constantly in the air during the hours of daylight, this is not done at present, owing to limitations set on the number of flying hours which each aircraft may perform. Auster aircraft, like many other things, are in short supply, and if they are to be available during a battle in the necessary numbers, economy must be practised now. The normal daily programme consists of four sorties, each of about 2½ hours duration. Each pilot is given a definite task to perform. This task is usually either to reconnoitre, or to shoot at targets allocated the evening before.

Each evening at 6 o'clock the duty pilot brings to HQ RA a report of the day's activities. He goes first to the CB office, where he sees on the daily shelling plot what enemy guns seem to have been active during the day, and discusses with the DCBO the best batteries for the Air OP to engage next morning. Two or three of the most active batteries will usually be selected for deliberate engagement with 155-mm or 8-inch howitzers.

Shoots of this type are carried out with a single gun, the object being to destroy as many pits as possible in the time available. As nothing short of a direct hit will achieve destruction, it may take anything up to eight or ten days' shooting to destroy a four-gun battery completely. At a time when ten or twenty positions are active daily, it will often be better to aim at the partial destruction of several positions than the complete destruction of one. In quieter periods, the Air OP may devote up to two days to the destruction of one gun position, carrying on systematically until each pit has received one or more direct hits. Some positions are provided with such excellent head cover that the first hit with an 8-inch shell will fail to penetrate, and further punishment has to be inflicted. All of which takes time and demands much skill and perseverance on the part of the pilots.

Apart from this mission of destruction, the Air OP may be briefed to reconnoitre objects which appear on air photographs to be possible gun positions, or to express an opinion on whether certain known gun positions are occupied or not. In the latter cases, the pilot's opinion will depend chiefly on whether men, or perhaps recent tracks, are seen on the position. Guns themselves are practically never seen from the air, due to camouflage and the solid head cover. The intelligence officer Royal Artillery (IO RA), too, may have tasks for the Air OP, such as a reconnaissance of targets for harassing fire, or the engagement of headquarters and supply dumps.

The flight commander is thus able to give each of his pilots a prearranged task, which he will carry out unless more important opportunity targets present themselves. If shelling starts, for instance, it is obviously better to deter a gun that is active than to carry on with the destruction of a gun that fired yesterday.

The drill to direct the attention of the Air OP to an active gun is usually as follows. Shells begin to land in an infantry locality. Within five minutes two or three shelreps have arrived in HQ RA. These normally reduce to one or two map squares in the area in which the hostile battery may be. The Air OP pilot is told to look in this area for an active enemy gun, in the hope that he will spot flashes. With any luck, he may be able to do this and at the same time continue to carry on the shoot in which he is engaged. If the targets are widely separated, it may be better to request a Corps Air OP to watch for flashes while our own pilot continues his shoot. A few moments later, a sound-ranging location may be made, narrowing down the area of search to a 200- or 300-yard circle. If there is a known position in this area, the Air OP will be told to take it on, whether he sees flashes or not. If there is no known position there the Air OP will go on looking for flashes, which is no easy task in the present circumstances, for the enemy normally fire a small number of rounds in irregular sequences from a large number of positions. In any case, they probably do everything possible to conceal the flash or smoke if they are using flashless ammunition, and may even time the firing of each round in accordance with the movement of the Air OP.

When a hate programme takes place the first battery to be located is usually taken on by our own Air OP, the second by a Corps Air OP and the third may be ranged on by the sound rangers doing a sound-on-sound shoot. Engagement in this case is intended as a deterrent, and consists of firing perhaps three or four volleys from a 155-mm six-gun battery – a comparatively quick process. A pilot may carry out two or even three such shoots during one sortie.

In addition to the counter-bombardment role, Air Ops will engage enemy in the open, using 25-pounders, and other worthwhile targets that cannot be seen properly from the ground.

In normal warfare, Air Ops usually have to fly behind our own forward defence lines (FDLs) not more than about 600 feet up. Here they normally fly at 4,000 to 5,000 feet, over enemy territory, and sometimes vertically over the targets they are engaging. At this height they are reasonably safe from AA machinegun fire, but not from 37-mm LAA guns, of which the enemy has about twenty or thirty within 10,000 yards of our Divisional FDLs. Fortunately, they are not usually aggressive, but if they do open fire they can be sure of engagement by field or medium artillery, probably using at least a proportion of variable time air-burst (VT) fuses. Their presence is a perpetual menace, and if they were allowed to go unpunished it would become extremely difficult to bring effective CB fire to bear on the greater part of the enemy gun area.

For reasons given earlier, it is not possible to have an aircraft in the air throughout the day (the gaps being filled in as far as possible by aircraft of 1913 Light Liaison Flight RAF), but there is always one available to go up at short notice should shelling start. Low clouds, high winds and poor visibility will also keep aircraft on the ground. When the Air OP Flight is earthbound, the CB staff is deprived of its most effective weapon.

The flight recently celebrated 2,000 hours of operational flying. May the next 2,000 be equally unpopular with the enemy gunners!

Annex III
Additional photographs

Chapter 3

Mia Jima

Self at Iwakuni

Mia Jima, sacred island in the Inland Sea

Annex III 99

Tokchong strip

100   Annex III

Number 4 Section and supporting cast

Pilot briefing: self on left, Major Ronnie Gower and Captain John Crawshaw

Waiting for the Boss to do a bad landing: Captains Dick Corfield and Leslie Addington and self on right

Chapter 5

Top: General Ridgeway, General Van Fleet, Lieutenant General O'Daniel arriving at Fort George strip; bottom left: Major-General Cassels briefing his masters on Operation Commando, 17 July 1951; bottom right: Major-General Cassels and Lieutenant General O'Daniel

Corsair finally ready for take-off

US Grumman Avenger landing and taking off from Fort George strip

Major-General Cassel's private aeroplane with RAF roundels and chauffeur, Captain Tony Wilson

Seoul City gateway   Korean woman making flour

Annex III 103

Joe Luscombe and I seem to have been invited in to the men's mess for a drink

LAC Howe and Gunner Price

Chapter 6

An American entertainer, Brigadier Pike and Danny Kaye

Chapter 8

Derek Jarvis

Ronnie Gower

Bob Warner

Arthur Stewart-Cox

Joe Luscombe and John Crawshaw

Gerry Joyce and Derek Jarvis

Brian Forward

Farewell drinks party for Major-General Cassels, at Divisional Headquarters

New Commander in Chief General Mark Clark and guard of honour of the King's Shropshire Light Infantry

King's Shropshire Light Infantry

King's Own Scottish Borderers

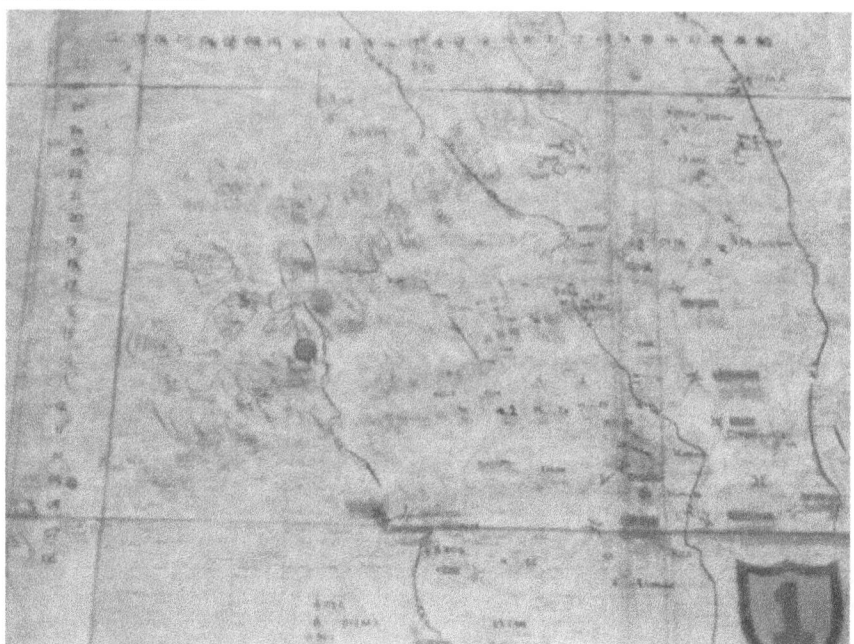

Divisional forward positions

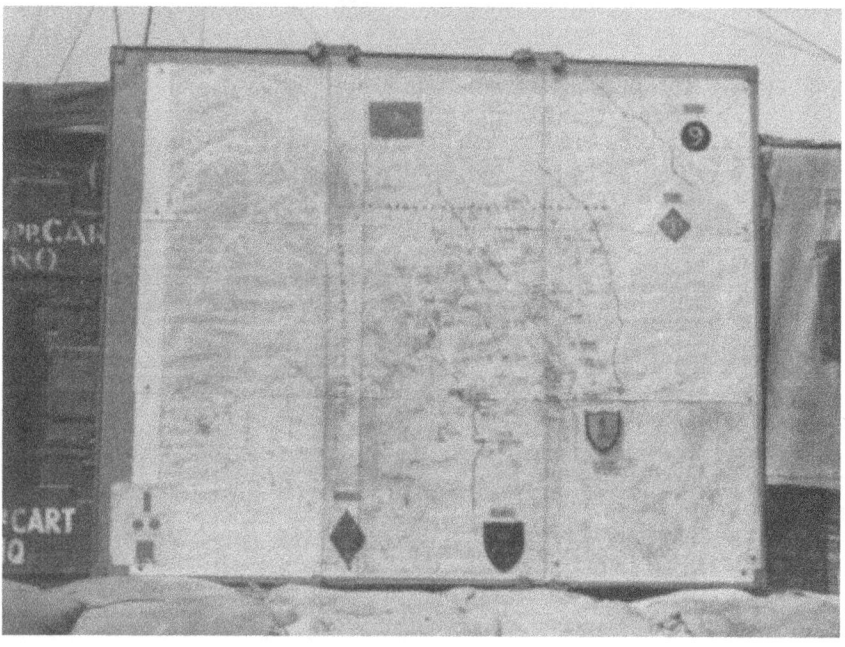

Battle maps

Annex III 107

Major-General Cassels briefing Selwyn Lloyd, General Van Fleet, Lord Alexander and General Clark

Selwyn Lloyd, Lord Alexander, Lieutenant-General O'Daniel

Guard of honour First Royal Canadian Regiment

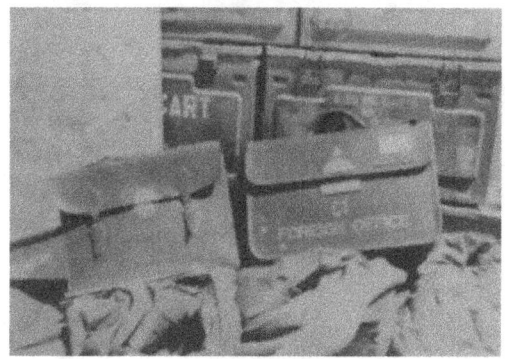

War Office briefcases

Major-General Cassels and Lord Alexander outside 1903 Flight Headquarters

108   Annex III

Kawana, near Tokyo   Kawana Golf Club

The sacred island of Mia Jima on the Inland Sea of Japan

Annex III 109

The sacred island of Mia Jima on the Inland Sea of Japan

Touring Japan

110 Annex III

Chapter 9

Right sector from the Observation Post

1st King's front; 75 Observation Post at top right

11 and 12 Platoons of B Company 1st King's from 75 Observation Post; enemy positions on point 166 and point 75 in the background the other side of the Samichon valley

The reverse slope of the company position and Gunner Jones outside the Observation Post base; the OP party consisted of Gunners Jones, the signaller, McColl, the driver/batman, and Parfitt, the OP assistant

Annex III

Reverse slope of B Company position

1st King's 3-inch mortars

Lieutenant-Colonel Jack Slade Powell **Captain John Painter E Troop, Major Tug Wilson Battery Commander, Captain Harry Pearson BK, and myself, F Troop**

Glossary

AA	anti-aircraft
AA LMG	anti-aircraft light machinegun
ALO	US air liaison officer
AOP	air observation post
B echelon	unit rear area where vehicles were kept
BC	battery commander
BCPO	battery command post officer
BMRA	brigade major Royal Artillery
C in C	commander in chief
Capt	captain
CB	counter-bombardment
CDN	Canadian
CCF	Chinese Communist forces
CO	commanding officer
Cpl	corporal
1st Comwel	1st Commonwealth Division
CRA	commander Royal Artillery
DCBO	divisional counter-bombardment officer
DFC	Distinguished Flying Cross
DSO	Distinguished Service Order
FA	936th Field Artillery Battalion
FDLs	forward defence lines
GPO	gun position officer
HAA	heavy anti-aircraft
HE	high explosive
HQ RA	Headquarters Royal Artillery
intreps	intelligence reports

Glossary

IO RA	intelligence officer Royal Artillery
KSLI	King's Shropshire Light Infantry
1st Kings	1st King's Liverpool Regiment
L19	American air OP aircraft, "Bird Dog"
LAA	Chinese 37-mm light anti-aircraft guns
LAC	leading aircraftsman
LMG	light machinegun
MIG	Russian built jet fighter
Maj	major
MC	Military Cross
OC	officer commanding
OP	observation post
"Persuader"	US 8-inch gun
RAA	Royal Australian Artillery
RAF	Royal Air Force
RAAF	Royal Australian Air Force
R&R	rest and recuperation
RSM	regimental sergeant-major
SAC	senior aircraftsman
shelreps	shelling reports
SOS	international distress call used to designate the targets of last resort
UN	United Nations
USAF	United States Air Force
VT	variable time air-burst fuse

www.ingramcontent.com/pod-product-compliance
Lightning Source LLC
Chambersburg PA
CBHW080519110426
42742CB00017B/3175